ALSO BY VIVEK WADHWA

*The Immigrant Exodus: Why America Is Losing the
Global Race to Capture Entrepreneurial Talent*

ALSO BY FARAI CHIDEYA

*Trust: Reaching the 100 Million Missing Voters
and Other Selected Essays*
The Color of Our Future: Race in the 21st Century
*Don't Believe the Hype: Fighting Cultural Misinformation
About African Americans*

Diversion Books
A Division of Diversion Publishing Corp.
443 Park Avenue South, Suite 1008
New York, New York 10016
www.DiversionBooks.com

For more information, email info@diversionbooks.com

First Diversion Books edition September 2014.
Print ISBN: 978-1-62681-422-6
eBook ISBN: 978-1-62681-383-0

INNOVATING WOMEN

The Changing Face of Technology

Vivek Wadhwa
& Farai Chideya

DIVERSIONBOOKS

CONTENTS

INTRODUCTION

At the 2009 TechCrunch Crunchies Awards—the Oscars of the tech industry—my wife, Tavinder, asked a question that confused me. "Vivek, do you notice something strange?"

"Yes," I whispered excitedly. "Mark Zuckerberg is sitting next to us."

She smiled indulgently and said, "Try again."

I looked around and said, "All the celebrities are dressed in ragged jeans and T-shirts?"

"No, Vivek," she said. *"Where are the women?"*

That one comment opened my eyes to an ugly reality: just as no women were featured on stage at the Crunchies other than the TechCrunch staff and one circus performer, the entire tech world was male-dominated. Suddenly I saw that the place I'd been touting as the world's greatest meritocracy had deep-rooted biases, which were systematically discriminating against the most innovative half of our population.

For years, I had been researching entrepreneurship, immigration, and what made Silicon Valley tick. With the help of noted academics, such as UC Berkeley dean AnnaLee Saxenian and Harvard economist Richard Freeman, my research teams at Duke University had published several groundbreaking academic papers. But I was so oblivious to the issue of gender that I didn't even record the sex of the thousands of entrepreneurs we had researched. Just as I hadn't noticed the gender gap at the TechCrunch event, it hadn't even occurred to me that there could be differences between male and female entrepreneurs.

I was ignorant.

I started looking at Silicon Valley from this new perspective, and I saw that the executive teams of the Valley's top tech firms had very few, if any, women technology heads. The entire management team of Apple didn't have a single woman. Virtually all of Silicon Valley's investment firms were male-dominated. The few women found on their websites were either in marketing or human resources. Venture capital firms, or VCs, were the worst offenders—of the eighty-nine VCs on the 2009 TheFunded.com list of top VCs, only one was a woman.

I began to take note of the myths and flaws and harmful stereotypes that are commonly propagated by the technology industry's power brokers. One such comment was from a legendary venture capitalist who I have always held in the highest regard and who I don't believe is sexist. Yet he said at a major conference:

> *In the early days, when you went back in the Amazon shipping area, the books were lined up so you could see what people were buying. Invariably there was a book about programming language like Java, and in the same sales order, there was a book like* The Joy of Sex. *These [customers] were probably very clearly male, nerds who had no social or sex lives trying to get help by using an online service.*
>
> *That correlates more with any other success factor that I've seen in the world's greatest entrepreneurs. If you look at [Amazon founder Jeff] Bezos, or [Netscape Communications Corporation founder Marc] Andreessen, [Yahoo! Inc. cofounder] David Filo, the founders of Google, they all seem to be white, male, nerds who've dropped out of Harvard or Stanford, and they absolutely have no social life. So when I see that pattern coming in—which was true of Google—it was very easy to decide to invest.*

There was no public outcry about these comments, no apology, no retraction. In other industries, there would have been an uproar, but in tech, discrimination on sex, race, and age was considered acceptable.

VCs commonly claimed they knew an entrepreneur when they saw one. And sadly, it was—and still is—acceptable for venture capitalists to openly tout their supposed "pattern recognition" abilities. But the patterns they saw were always young, white, male nerds resembling the founders above—and the VCs themselves. As such, "pattern recognition" is nothing more than a legitimized way of discriminating against women and minorities, which has no place in business or society in this day and age.

There is *innovation*—the spark that prompts an idea, concept, or company. And then there is *implementation*—which requires capital. And that is what skews the gender balance even more. Implementing ideas has—so far—required significant amounts of capital. Venture capitalists have controlled access to this capital.

As tech guru and angel investor Esther Dyson explains, "VCs tend to invest in people who look like themselves, whether it's color, whether it's gender, whether it's social class. It's hard to know who can be successful, so they tend to work with the familiar, and that leaves out most women," she said.

To get a better understanding of the root of the gender problem, I decided to reanalyze data from my own studies on entrepreneurship. I did web searches and made phone calls to verify the gender of several hundred entrepreneurs whom my team had researched, and I was surprised to learn that there was virtually no difference between successful male and female entrepreneurs. Their motivations were practically identical, as were their education levels, success factors, and reasons for starting a business. They had even learned the same lessons from their past successes and failures.

The only difference was that women placed a higher value than men did on their business partners and on their personal and professional networks. This made me wonder whether women were really cut out for the rough-and-tumble, self-involved world of entrepreneurship. So I reviewed data[1] from the Kauffman Foundation, which showed that women were actually more

[1] "Sources of Financing for New Technology Firms: A Comparison by Gender," Kauffman Foundation, July 2009, http://www.kauffman. org/what-we-do/research/kauffman-firm-survey-series/sources-of-financing-for-new-technology-firms-a-comparison-by-gender

capital-efficient than men. Babson's Global Entrepreneurship Monitor[2] revealed that women-led, high-tech startups had lower failure rates than those led by men.

I then considered whether a difference in educational backgrounds could be a factor. Not at all, I learned. Data from the National Science Foundation[3] showed that girls now matched boys in mathematical achievement. In the United States alone, 140 women enrolled in higher education for every 100 men. Women earned more than 50 percent of all bachelor's and master's degrees and nearly 50 percent of all doctorates.

This led me to address the gender imbalance in a regular blog that I was writing for TechCrunch in 2010, "Silicon Valley: You and Some of Your VCs have a Gender Problem."[4] I was surprised at the intensity of the response I received in a barrage of hate mail, immature online chatter, and personal attacks on me over Twitter. I was further stunned to receive e-mails from highly respected VCs—who I *used* to call my friends. One asked what my "agenda" was in bringing up an issue like this. Another warned that "this was not the way to achieve success in the Valley." Another asked whether I was "trying to get laid" and suggested there were "better ways."

A month later, a prominent Silicon Valley investor tweeted that he "disagree[s] with [all] TC [TechCrunch] posts I've ever read by Vivek Wadhwa" and that "his posts are garbage." One investor tweeted: "mystified that he gets visibility & access to public platforms - has anyone ever tested his positions? Watch him on bloomberg. Lawd!" Another wrote, "He is misrepresenting the data. And that is why he is a loser" and "no, he is a fraud."

Being new to Silicon Valley and having already been embroiled in nasty debates with nativists over my research on and supportive views of skilled immigration, I was reluctant to

---

[2] http://www.gemconsortium.org/docs/download/2825

[3] Global Entrepreneurship Monitor 2012 Women's Report http://www.nsf.gov/statistics/wmpd/2013/tables.cfm

[4] Vivek Wadhwa, "Silicon Valley: You and Some of Your VC's have a Gender Problem." *TechCrunch*, February 7, 2010. http://techcrunch.com/2010/02/07/silicon-valley-you've-got-a-gender-problem-and-some-of-your-vc's-still-live-in-the-past/

pick a fight with Silicon Valley's moguls. Tavinder and I had just decided to move permanently to the Bay area, and I didn't want to make enemies in my new home. She had sacrificed her own career so that she could support mine and had been by my side through all of my ups and downs. When I had a life-threatening heart attack in 2002, the doctors weren't sure whether I would make it, but she wouldn't let me die. She stayed at my bedside in the ICU, not sleeping, for three and a half days. She is the secret of my success and the person I go to whenever I have any ethical or moral dilemmas. After my heart attack, the doctors didn't want me to go back to my stressful job as CEO of a technology company, so Tavinder insisted I do something else I was passionate about. I decided to teach and become a mentor to students. I would be earning a fraction of my former salary, but she said we would downsize and manage with less. And on the women-in-technology front, she gave me clear marching orders.

"Vivek," she said, "if you feel badly about the attacks you are enduring, imagine how the women feel: they have to live with them every day. You must wage this battle with them. If you don't, who will?"

It did not take much encouragement for me to fight for this important cause. Over the past five years, I've written dozens of articles about the dearth of women in technology and interviewed more than 400 female entrepreneurs. I also just concluded a new research study for which my team at Stanford University surveyed and interviewed more than 500 women in technology from all around the globe. The results, published by the Kauffman Foundation, indicated that there had been distinct changes in attitudes over time—women were becoming more confident and assertive, and they were helping each other out. They were even being mentored and coached by men. There was still a lot of work to be done to bridge the gender gap, but things were moving in the right direction.

But academic papers are always boring. You get frowned upon for expressing any opinion whatsoever. So I decided to write a book for the general reader. I had already made a considerable personal investment in the research, but when

I went to get Tavinder's buy-in to spend another $35,000, her response intrigued me.

"Why don't you get women to fund this book and volunteer to write it? If they really appreciate what you're doing for them, they will surely help you!" she said.

That was when a light switched on in my head and the idea to crowdfund and crowdcreate the book materialized. After all, what right did I—a male—have to tell women how to solve their problems? I might understand the source of it, but I wasn't particularly qualified to prescribe remedies. I estimated that I would need another $40,000 to pay Neesha, hire a journalist to curate the content, and pay for the book's campaign and infrastructure. I guessed that I would need at least thirty or forty female participants in order for the text to have real depth and breadth.

To that end, I sent a message to my private mailing list, asking whether any women wanted to work with me. I was delighted when legendary journalist and TV anchor Farai Chideya wrote back immediately, offering to help in any way she could—as did dozens of other women. Some of my male friends said that since they were disqualified from participating, they would encourage their wives and daughters to get involved. I was flooded with pledges of unqualified support from nearly everyone I knew, including my colleagues at Singularity University—Ray Kurzweil, Peter Diamandis, and Rob Nail.

One of the first things I did was ask some of our women supporters to sign up as "ambassadors," to spread the word and get women to sign up as coauthors. I was hoping to attract ten or twenty ambassadors. I was delighted to gather more than 300. Instead of the thirty coauthors I had hoped for, we now had more than 500. They shared ideas and told us their stories, and we brainstormed the ways in which they could uplift other female entrepreneurs. They provided us with more information than we could have accumulated in years of research. This book is the result of their efforts—which Farai Chideya has helped elegantly synthesize.

Vivek Wadhwa, 2014
Moffett Field, California

CHAPTER 1
THE GROWING SUCCESS OF
INNOVATING WOMEN

Innovating Women dives into a series of issues and inflection points that dictate how quickly a woman's participation in the innovation society grows. Each chapter presents a different facet of the challenge and opportunity and includes essays from "innovating women." This is not just a book; it's a flag planted in the ground—a declaration of interdependence by the hundreds of women who contributed to this crowdcreated volume. All of them are involved in innovation and entrepreneurship, particularly in the fields of STEM (science, technology, engineering, and mathematics). Using an online platform as well as individual interviews, we collected the wisdom of pioneers from dozens of countries. In turn, by sharing their stories, the author-participants discovered a powerful sense of belonging and recognition.

Quendrith Johnson, the founder and executive producer of Screenmancer, an online portal for filmmakers, said, "This project, through the threads and minds of all these various women, all exceptional in my view, has sort of brought me to the realization of how much of my STEM self is hidden on a daily basis. It is a watershed most likely not just for me but for everyone involved."

Innovation rises from inspiration. Take the case of Kay Koplovitz. As an American college student visiting London in the 1960s, she saw a poster for a lecture on geosynchronous orbiting satellites. While many students would have been on their way to a pub or a concert, she was thinking, "What an intriguing topic!" Space had fascinated her ever since the Russians had launched Sputnik into orbit.

"He spoke with such passion," Koplovitz said of the man on stage—famed science fiction writer, Arthur C. Clarke, the author of *2001: A Space Odyssey*. Clarke had served as a radar specialist for the British Army during World War II. He described geosynchronous orbiting satellites positioned 22,300 miles above the Earth—rendering them stationary over a fixed location—as being ideal vehicles for global communications.

Koplovitz had interned as a television producer during her college years. When she became aware of this new tool, she saw commercial opportunities—and freedom.

"One has to remember that this was the time of the Cold War," Koplovitz said. "It was a time of international espionage and intrigue. Most of us didn't know that much about what was going on behind the Berlin Wall or the Great Wall of China. And I thought: 'Wow, it would be really wonderful if we could communicate with the people behind those walls.'

"Back then, we had three broadcast networks in the United States. People thought that was a lot," she laughed. "The idea of using satellites for commercial, rather than military, purposes seemed far-fetched, but that's what Arthur C. Clarke had inspired me to envision—I wanted to fulfill that dream of actually being able to connect with people."

And so, in 1977, Koplovitz founded Madison Square Garden Sports, the predecessor to the USA Network, and then the SyFy Channel in 1992. She negotiated all the first deals to bring professional sports to cable. Major League Baseball was the first, followed closely by the National Basketball Association, the National Hockey League, the Masters Golf Tournament, and the U.S. Tennis Open.

As if her entrepreneurial accomplishments weren't enough, Koplovitz went on to help other women succeed, cofounding Springboard Enterprises, which showcased women-led companies for a select group of investors. Among the female-led companies for which she helped secure funding is iRobot, which produced the Roomba automated vacuum. The company generated $436 million in revenue in 2012. Her grit and determination and her willingness to champion other women in science, technology, and innovation was part of a seismic shift in our business landscape and global society.

Some women have been fortunate enough to amass the resources to directly incentivize the long-overdue gender integration of technology fields. Lynn Tilton runs Patriarch Partners, a holding company with eight billion dollars of revenue. I had her invited to an event at the X Prize Foundation, which is affiliated with Singularity University, the entrepreneurial think tank where I am a fellow. [X Prizes are a series of multimillion-dollar awards for top innovators.]

"I'd say I felt like I was coming home," Tilton said, "because it was a group of people who were there to really focus on making the world a better place…less so on pushing their own wares and agenda…more on how to combine our minds to change the world."

Teaming up with me and former Michigan governor Jennifer Granholm, among others, Tilton gave $5 million to fund a second-tier prize available only to X Prize winners. The X2 Prize was an additional monetary award for any future X Prize-winning team whose leadership boasts a female CEO and has at least 50 percent women—dubbed "The Mother of All Prizes."

"It really comes down to men understanding that they are much better off with women by their side," Tilton said. "Including women on top management teams really creates a much more successful enterprise. But until men realize that and embrace it, nothing is going to change. I wanted X2 to go to any winning X Prize team so that team after team after team would be incentivized to bring women to the leadership level from the start. That was my thought process—maybe money would be the reason to [integrate] the teams, and then that configuration would be the key to winning the prize."

Clearly, extraordinary efforts are being made to raise the fortunes of women in innovation. But what we know now is that the inclusion of women has a positive impact. A study by

Catalyst found that: "Companies with the highest representation of women on their top management teams experienced better financial performance than companies with the lowest women's representation. This finding held for both financial measures analyzed: Return on Equity (ROE), which is 35 percent higher, and Total Return to Shareholders (TRS), which is 34 percent higher."[5]

Still, much evidence exists to show that women were hardly getting a fair shake. According to the firm Startup Compass, "Only 10 percent of Internet entrepreneurs across the world are women."[6] And yet women innovators today, despite being underrepresented, are rising in influence and achieving transformative gains for society. They are not waiting for men to create a level playing field, although many men are supporters and allies.

Alec Ross, the former senior advisor for innovation at the State Department and the architect of "digital diplomacy" asserts that if American women participated in the labor market at the same level as men did, the gross domestic product (GDP) would be 8 percent higher.[7] If we, as a global society, allowed women to shine, it would improve our economies, our quality of life, and the range of opportunities for women and girls. And those gains would be even greater in some developing countries. Every day, women innovators stake their success on their own ideas and hard work. They come from diverse backgrounds and put themselves on the line as they build new technologies, often taking on huge societal challenges in the process.

And then there are what might gently be called gender attitude problems in the workplace. We reported in a new research paper, published by the Kauffman Foundation, that 85 percent

---

[5] "Connecting Corporate Performance and Gender Disparity," Catalyst, 2004; "Sources of Financing for New Technology Firms: A Comparison by Gender," Kauffman Foundation, http://www.kauffman.org/what-we-do/research/kauffman-firm-survey-series/sources-of-financing-for-new-technology-firms-a-comparison-by-gender.

[6] "The Middle East Beats the West in Female Tech Founders," *The Economist*, July 13, 2013.

[7] Cited by Ross: "Women's Work: Driving the Economy," The Goldman Sachs Group, Inc., April 25, 2013.

of female entrepreneurs feel their work environment favors men, and 41 percent blame social and cultural issues for preventing their female colleagues from launching their own startups.[8]

As Quendrith Johnson explained, "Anyone familiar with the film *The Social Network* has watched the scene where Mark Zuckerberg is encouraged to print '*I'm the CEO, bitch,*' on his Facebook business cards. That said everything about gender. If you are lucky enough to be a female CEO, there is a 100 percent chance you have been called a bitch! So, my approach was to put that on the table, but not as a pejorative. My favorite comeback is, '*I've got a PhD in Bitch. Next?*'"

Another one of our collaborators, Rashmi Nigam, a product manager in Los Angeles, raises the issue of discrimination based on stereotypes about working mothers. Despite arriving in the office at 5:30 a.m. and working twelve-hour days, Nigam's boss at a previous company criticized her for working "mommy hours." In some technological environments, particularly among coders, arriving at the office later in the day is not seen as a detriment, but leaving "early"—at the time most American workers go home—is perceived as a negative.

We're not here to sugarcoat the challenges facing women in technology, but we're not going to wallow in them either. Despite the gender biases in the innovation industries, the meaningful participation of women stands poised for substantial growth. Exponential technologies like 3-D printing, advances in robotics, and the rapidly dropping costs of processing power and data storage have dramatically lowered the cost of starting a business. Arguably, the advent of social media played to the strengths of women as connectors. In the case of Koplovitz and Springboard, women who'd already made it to the top were now extending a ladder for yet more female innovators to climb. It remained to be seen whether the growth of women innovators and their companies will be briskly incremental or hockey stick exponential, but there is no question that the world is ready for women to lead us into the future.

---

[8] Upcoming report from Kauffman Foundation by Vivek Wadhwa et al. on "The changing face of Silicon Valley."

Women Are the Great Disruptors

WHITNEY JOHNSON

Whitney Johnson is the cofounder of Rose Park Advisors, an investment firm built on the principles of disruptive innovation. She is a regular contributor to the Harvard Business Review, *a* TEDx *speaker, and a prolific tweeter on startups and investments.*

I discovered the theory of disruptive innovation in 2004, when I heard Clayton Christensen speak about "The Innovator's Dilemma." As a sell-side analyst at Merrill Lynch, covering telecom and media in the emerging markets, I immediately recognized that Christensen's theory explained why mobile penetration was repeatedly beating my estimates—mobile was disrupting fixed-line telephony.

The more familiar I became with Christensen's frameworks, the more I was convinced that these ideas were just as applicable to individuals—and to me, in particular—as they were to industry. At the time, I had been an institutional investor-ranked sell-side analyst for nearly a decade. I was at the top of my game, but I wanted to make more of a dent in the universe. Theoretically, if I stayed at Merrill Lynch, that wasn't going to happen. To upend my status quo, I would need to play where no one else was playing.

Within a few months, I quit my job to become an entrepreneur. Many colleagues questioned my sanity. For me, getting to that place of power and respect was hard-won. I had started out as a secretary, moved up the food chain into investment banking, and became an award-winning analyst. Why would I walk away to try my hand at writing a children's book and produce a reality TV show about Latin America? (Neither of which happened, by the way.) Instead, I ended up blogging about work/life issues for *Harvard Business Review* and cofounding an investment fund with Clay Christensen. To colleagues and friends, these career moves might have seemed wanton, but when you considered them within the framework of disruptive innovation (the most successful innovations are those that create new markets and value networks, thereby upending existing ones), my career switch made perfect sense.

Lest you think my entrepreneurial stint had been one straight shot up the y-axis of success, let me set the record straight. There have been many times when it was lonely and scary. After the adrenaline rush of quitting my job in 2005 wore off, there were days when I felt a total loss of identity. I could no longer call people and say, "Whitney Johnson, Merrill Lynch." Those words used to validate me. Now it was just "Whitney Johnson," and sometimes that wasn't enough. There were days when my P/E (Puke/Excitement) ratio was so uncomfortably high that it felt like I was on a thrill ride to zero cash flow—as when I backed a business in 2006 that was initially successful, but then failed miserably. Almost by definition, there was that sense of unfamiliarity. If you were playing where no one else was playing, at the outset you felt completely alone.

I was confident that many women who were pushing the envelope of innovation, especially in science and technology, had similar feelings. Between 2000 and 2008, there was a 79 percent decline in the number of incoming undergraduate women majoring in computer science. In 2009, 57 percent of college grads were women, yet only 18 percent of them had computer science degrees. Our society was continuing to project a message that women wouldn't fit in or didn't have a place in technology. The entrenched stereotype of a "coder" was the geeky white male. It wasn't easy to fight stereotypes, but doing the unexpected was exactly what disruption was all about.

Our world will continue to be driven by technology, and we simply cannot afford to leave women out in the cold. Women bring unique talents and perspectives to the table in any field, but they are particularly vital to a world of invention and innovation shaped by technology. What amazing products, processes, and bold leaps of thinking would we all miss out on if women couldn't choose to disrupt the status quo? What if we were forcing some of our most brilliant minds away from technology? I personally do not want to live in a world created entirely by men!

Though it might be lonely and scary, here are three good reasons for disrupting yourself:

1. If, in the deepest part of your nature, you know that you must disrupt and you don't, you'll die just a little inside. Hence, what we call the Innovator's Dilemma—whether you innovate or not, you risk downward mobility.

2. The odds of success are six times higher (up from 6 percent to 36 percent—so you still might fail, but the odds are tilted significantly in your favor) and the revenue opportunity is twenty times greater when you pursue a disruptive course.

3. As a woman, you have a disruptive edge. When conducting research on why women changed jobs more successfully than men, Harvard Business School professor Boris Groysberg learned: "Women build networks outside their organization that remain intact when they leave...Not because women set out to [do this], but because they are often marginalized, left out of the internal power structure...they build external networks out of necessity." In other words, women instinctively know how to play where no one else is playing.

Bottom line: If you want to unleash innovation, hire a woman. Better yet, invest in or start up a woman-led company.

According to a Dow Jones study, successful venture capital-backed companies have, on average, two times more women in the highest ranks. Indeed, these companies have a greater chance of either going public, turning a profit, or being sold for more money than they've raised.

We give a lot of airtime to building and buying disruptive companies. But I believe that harnessing this powerful mindset begins with the individual: companies don't disrupt, people do. If you really want to disrupt the status quo, follow the advice of former British Prime Minister Margaret Thatcher, and "go ask a woman."

Innovating Women
in History

A 2012 Google doodle of a woman drawing mathematical equations with a quill pen was the first introduction many people had to Ada Lovelace, seen by some as the first computer programmer. According to the British Science Museum, Lovelace saw that the "punched card input device, the Analytical Engine, opened up a whole new opportunity for designing machines that could manipulate symbols rather than just numbers. Her achievements were even more exceptional given the attitudes of Victorian Britain toward the intellectual pursuits of women."[9] That was in 1843. It took another century before work like hers was even put into public use. More recently, we've seen innovators like Anita Borg, who began as a programmer in 1969 and taught herself to code and work on projects such as e-mail and online community platforms. Borg founded the Institute for Women and Technology, and since she passed away in 2003, the group has borne her name: The Anita Borg Institute for Women and Technology.[10] But our foray into history unfortunately shows regress as well as progress—for example, the percentage of female programmers was actually higher in the 1980s than it is today.[11][12] Progress often takes the

[9] "Ada Lovelace," Science Museum, http://www.sciencemuseum.org.uk/onlinestuff/stories/ada_lovelace.aspx.

[10] Anita Borg, "Where We Are and Where We Are Going," Anita Borg Institute for Women and Technology, 1993.

[11] Tracy Camp, "Women in Computer Sciences: Reversing the Trend," Colorado School of Mines, August 2001.

[12] Claire Cain Miller, "In Google's Inner Circle, a Falling Number of Women," *The New York Times*, August 22, 2012.

form of two steps forward, one step backward, yet still remains a forward march toward inclusion.

We tapped into our deep well of contributors and found an amazing array of experiences with STEM education—from having outstanding parents and extraordinary teachers to school systems and peer groups that exhibited disturbing gender bias.

Priyanka Pathak, a technologist and ICT innovation specialist at the World Bank, said, "It's funny because as a kid, I would never have believed that I would end up working in tech, or any STEM field for that matter. My father is an accomplished materials scientist, and while I maintained a 4.0 grade point average throughout high school, nobody ever disagreed with me whenever I said I didn't think I was that good at math or science. On the contrary, someone usually suggested that I use my personality, language skills, and communication skills to pursue another career path instead. My calculus teacher joked that I was 'too sociable' to ever study anything in STEM, my physics teacher once made fun of my not-so-great test scores in front of the entire class, my MIT admissions interviewer point-blank told me that I would never fit in at MIT because I had a social life, and my chemistry teacher asked why on Earth I didn't get an A on the final exam when I had a scientist father! All this subtle messaging convinced me not only that I was dumb when it came to math and science, but also that unless I wanted to be a doctor (which I didn't), STEM was only for people who wanted to program computers, solve mathematical equations, or pour chemicals in a corner somewhere for their entire lives, which sounded extremely unappealing anyway." How can we identify the different factors that lead women and girls away from science, math, engineering, and technology? A 2010 study by Bayer Corporation examined whether minorities and women were actively discouraged from pursuing STEM careers. 60 percent said yes, and most of the discouragement occurred at college; 44 percent said that college professors were usually the source of the negative feedback. 77 percent said that the workforce was lacking in minority and female applicants because these groups were never encouraged or nurtured to achieve in

STEM. 75 percent attributed the lack of diversity to the lack of quality science and math programs in poorer school districts.[13] However, once women left the arena of early and college STEM education, entry into the field could take many other routes—via graduate school, internships, or jobs. But any sort of bias could unsettle anyone early in their careers.

"How does a young scientist gain defiance, bravery, chutzpah, and audacity?" asked Susan Baxter, executive director of the California State University Program for Education and Research in Biotechnology. "On my very first job as a scientist, I arrived early at work to set up my presentation. Just then, the big-big-big boss arrived and asked me where the coffee was located and wherever it was, could I get some for him? Even in 1986, this was pretty surprising! I was a bit defiant and muttered that I had no idea how to help him on either front. Later that morning, when I was called to the stage, I could see that the big-big-big boss was quite surprised—I was part of a large, award-winning product launch team (my male supervisor fought tooth and nail for me to get that award), and I was quite proud."

And once women rooted down in their professions, decisions became even more complex. The Anita Borg Institute for Women and Technology and the Michael R. Clayman Institute for Gender Research at Stanford conducted a study of female scientists and engineers at seven mid-to-large publicly traded Silicon Valley high-tech firms. The study found that women at the mid-level stage were at "perhaps the most critical juncture" in their careers because that was where a complex set of gender barriers converged. Many mid-level women alluded to a "family penalty." Some delayed childbearing or even chose not to marry or have children in order to remain on their career track. And when it came to support, the report said, "Mid-level men were almost four times more likely than women to have a partner who assumed the primary responsibility for the

---

[13] "Bayer Facts of Science Education XIV: Female and Minority Chemists and Chemical Engineers Speak About Diversity and Underrepresentation in STEM," Bayer Corporation, March 2010.

household and children."[14]

What happens to an innovator when her work is critically important, but she is also the sole or primary parent in her family? Alice Rathjen, CEO and founder of *DNA Guide*, a genome-mapping software company, said, "I'm a single parent with a ten-year-old boy. The secret to survival for me was to find a core group of parents who helped each other out. One of the big advantages of giving and asking for help with daycare is that you bond with more kids than your own and share with others the joy of watching the whole group grow up together."

Feben Yohannes, the cofounder at GlobalStudent Social said, "The never-ending juggling act that we do as mothers is overwhelming at times, but that process, if channeled properly, is what makes us a creative, resourceful, and dynamic bunch." She is the single parent of a twelve-year-old whom she has raised on her own since her child was one. She's also an immigrant without much family living near her in the United States. "I have come to rely on friends and my community for support," she said. "About three years ago, a group of us started a young mother's association where we meet once a month to ensure that our kids bond and we strengthen our support system. We have a monthly contribution that is set aside for any emergencies. This group and additional other friends have been a huge support in caring for my daughter during my travels."

Even women with spouses or partners find that being an innovator and raising children are not incompatible. Both require the same level of dexterity and innovation as they normally apply to their work.

Facebook Chief Operating Officer Sheryl Sandberg's bestseller *Lean In* became a reference point for women evaluating their own decision-making. As Srijata Bhatnagar, senior product manager at 10kinfo Data Solutions puts it, "To me, leaning in really means understanding your potential, your choices, and your capabilities, and then taking defined, informed steps to

---

[14] "Climbing the Technical Ladder," Anita Borg Institute for Women and Technology and the Michael R. Clayman Institute for Gender Research at Stanford University, 2008.

'reclaim your life' based on your preferences."

Anne Hartley, who began her programming career in 1976 and is now the principal consultant at AH Consulting, added, "I interpret *Lean In* to mean engaging with your full capability and potential. Although the themes and examples in Sheryl's book are messages for women in the workplace, I think the call-to-action is at a higher level of consciousness—applied by both women and men in the pursuit of life and what we choose to make of it and the impact we feel compelled to strive for."

In order to understand how far we've come, let's take a walk through the life cycle of a woman innovator. First comes education, then the first rungs of the career ladder, followed by the mid-career years, when women who have already proven themselves are most likely to leave the field.[15] One reason they do, but certainly not the only reason, is that women choosing to start a family have to then dual-track their attentions to children and work. Women who want to become entrepreneurs after working for established companies heighten their level of risk, but sometimes find entrepreneurship more flexible and more suited to their lifestyle if they have families. Other women at this same mid-career juncture, who have built up resources or gained key positions in venture capital firms, become investors, thus renewing the cycle of growth.

And with innovation and implementation being different phases of an entrepreneur's life, growing a company to scale has to rely on rounds of funding that sometimes preserve the downside of entrepreneurship—the risk of inconsistently being able to support yourself or your family, with less and less of the upside of success like a return after dilution of equity. Companies achieving a return are based on private-ownership profitability, i.e. a successful initial public offering (IPO), or the ability to sell the company in an acquisition (like Waze, the social navigation firm, which had several women on its leadership team and sold

---

[15] Catherine Ashcraft and Sarah Blithe, "Women in IT: The Facts," National Center for Women & Information Technology, 2009; updated April 2010.

to Google for $966 million in 2013[16]). But before any of that is an option, many companies have to seek additional funding in order to reach a wide enough market to be competitive.

The birth of Springboard Enterprises in 1999 is a case in point. It started as a simple call for women founders to present their businesses to investors.

"We had [to appease] the naysayers. So that first year, we were hoping to get a hundred applications; by the time the deadline arrived, we had 350. And we were like, holy cow, what are we going to do with 350 paper applications?"

Assisted by several MBA students, the group chose twenty-six companies to present to investors in January 2000. Sixty days later, the tech market crashed.

"We're going forward," Koplovitz told her colleagues. "Last in, first out…that's not going to happen to us."

Twenty-two of the twenty-six companies received funding that first go-round. To date, Springboard had helped 550 companies get off the ground, and Koplovitz claims that out of close to five thousand companies she'd seen, 83 percent of them raised capital through Springboard, and 80 percent *of those* are still in business today, more than thirteen years later. Close to a third had positive liquidity events for their investors, including ten IPOs.

Springboard is not alone. "There are quite a few of these investment clubs, if you want to call them that," Koplovitz said. "Golden Seeds, Belle Capital, Phenomenal, Women's Capital Fund, and 37 Angels. There are really many, many of these angel clubs out there, all of which are looking to fund young companies. Quite a few of them are focused on investing in women-led businesses because their investors are primarily women (and also current or former entrepreneurs themselves). It's a virtuous circle that guys have controlled for a long time, and now it's time for women to have their turn. But we still need to concentrate on supporting women entrepreneurs. We still have a lot of ground to make up, even though we are making progress."

[16] Dan Graziano, "Google Finally Discloses Waze Acquisition Price," http://bgr.com/2013/07/26/google-waze-acquisition-price/

Early On

SIAN MORSON

Sian Morson is an entrepreneur and author. In 2010, Sian founded Kollective Mobile to help other businesses and startups with mobile development and strategy. She currently oversees operations and leads all business development and strategic efforts. Sian is also the author of Learn Design of iOS Development *and the forthcoming* Learn Design of Android Development.

I'm not new to technology, but I definitely took a long way to get to where I am today. As a young girl in junior high school in the Bronx, I remember having a computer lab where Mr. Fuller, an African-American, taught us about computers and BASIC. I was fascinated with the way things worked back then, and I still am to this day. That fascination led me to ask my parents for a Commodore VIC 20 and later a Commodore 64 to expand my budding interest in technology. I didn't think then, nor do I now, that there was anything wrong with being a young black girl programming software on the living room floor of her mother's Bronx apartment a few years after arriving in the United States. I realize, however, just how rare that scenario is and how unlikely it would be today.

I don't have a "struggle" story to tell. My story is not one of luck or being in the right place at the right time. It is one of hard work, determined perseverance, passion, and intuition.

In 1997, I met my friend James in San Francisco in a dive bar called Liquid. He was tall with long black hair shaved at the sides, rode a motorcycle, and wore a black leather jacket. He was impatient, smoked like a chimney, and drank too much. He was the first software engineer I'd ever met and the person who taught me HTML. He also had the coolest apartment I'd ever seen, with a room filled with computers. Over tequila shots and Camel Lights, he showed me my first online web page I'd ever seen, and within a few months, he gave me my first computer that connected to the Internet—it was a 386 with dial-up, had Netscape for a browser, and was running something called Visual Page by Symantec. Life would never be the same. We are still friends to this day.

My knowledge of HTML helped me get my first job at a startup called LookSmart in San Francisco, and after that, I went on to become a project manager at McCann Erickson and expanded my knowledge of technology by managing large-scale web builds for clients like MGM, Coca-Cola, and Philips. There was no one that looked like me for a very long time as I moved up the ranks. Not at CNET or at any of the other technology companies, and not even when I moved back into advertising. I learned to adjust. Black women at the agencies I worked at were in HR or some other administrative or supporting roles. There weren't any obvious examples of outright bias that I can recall, and I moved up quickly. But there were no role models either. No one took me under their wing and showed me the ropes, and if they did, they looked more like James than like me. I carved my own path up the ladder of success, buoyed by the beliefs instilled in me by my family and by having a strong sense of self.

THE IPHONE

In June of 2007, the iPhone was announced, and again the tech landscape shifted. Back then, I was working at the number one independent health-care agency in the United States as director of Interactive. I'd just returned from London, where I'd earned my master's degree in electronic arts from Middlesex University. I was restless and had already had a taste of the future and what mobile could do while I was in Europe. I knew that mobile was the future.

I shared my enthusiasm with my then-CEO, and within a year, I was heading up a new, mobile-specific division of the company and was looking to hire a team of iOS developers, account managers, project managers, engineers, and QA—all reporting to me. Turns out that the mobile thing had legs after all. The subsidiary, called EV2, was successful. Board members were happy, and we were bringing in more business than we could deliver. But like all entrepreneurs, I grew restless. The entrepreneurial spirit, for those of you who know it, never lets you rest. You're constantly buzzing with new ideas, and the muse never lets you be. And so after growing the business, I decided to step out again. I could have stayed. I was very comfortable. But my grandmother, a strong, big-boned "island woman" who never went to college, instilled in me the power of believing in my intuition. I followed that intuition right out of my cushy C-level job and into my own agency, and I haven't looked back since.

I used savings to bootstrap the mobile agency that would become Kollective Mobile. I had no idea how I would get clients, work, employees, or even make money. But I did know that I knew how to build a mobile business from the ground up. I'd done it before, and I'd do it again. I also knew that the traditional agency model had to change. Having cut my teeth at some of the top advertising agencies in the world, I knew how agencies pitched and won new business, how they staffed accounts, and most importantly how they managed projects. Most agencies are top-heavy with highly paid "strategists" and account managers. At the time, very little time or energy was spent on how the work got done. The traditional waterfall method was failing in the face of new technologies and methodologies. I wanted to try something smaller, leaner, and more agile.

KOLLECTIVE MOBILE

In October of 2010, I proudly opened Kollective Mobile for business. I was running the business from the living room of my small Oakland apartment. Having an agency background, I naturally tapped that resource for prospective clients. And I tapped some of the talented engineers and designers I'd met along the way to come and work with me.

It wasn't that difficult—agencies, for the most part, missed the mobile boat. They didn't see it coming. Many of the larger ones had invested lots of time and money convincing clients to build Flash banners and websites and paying "Flash technologists" to create them. Within a few years of the arrival of the iPhone, Flash started its inevitable decline, never to recover.

Kollective Mobile's first clients were and still are a collection of agencies, entrepreneurs, and startups. We work with them to understand the ever-shifting mobile landscape and to craft a mobile strategy that works for them. I'm happy to say the agencies are now aware of how important mobile is.

As the CEO, I am personally involved in every project that we take on. I am usually responsible for the business development and all operations. But the project management bug just won't leave me alone. I've made it a practice to personally manage every new project that comes into the company. It keeps me sharp and ensures our clients that they are getting the very best that we have to offer. I am still friends with James, the impatient curmudgeon who in 1997 introduced me to the web and gave me that computer. In fact, most of my staff looks more like James than me. At Kollective Mobile, I'm one of two women and the only person of color. I hope this changes soon with initiatives encouraging more women, girls, and people of color to code. But for now, I'm happy to be here.

Toward this end, I threw my own hat into the ring and opened Kollective South, a coworking space and community tech center in Atlanta, Georgia. I hope to be able to do my part in bridging the digital divide and bringing technology to underserved communities.

Being involved with mobile has taken me onto the stages at Modev, SXSW, and in front of hundreds of students at Ohio University. Last year, I was approached by Apress to write a book on iOS design. *Learn Design for iOS Development* hit Amazon at

Christmas of last year and continues to sell well. This summer, I'm beginning *Learn Design for Android* as well.

When I look back, I feel a great sense of accomplishment, but I'd rather look ahead at all the great things to come.

Here we begin our journey of discovery within the existing realm of accomplishments by women in technology and innovation. By following their ideas and dreams, we can create a pathway for generations of women to come.

CHAPTER 2
WOMAN TO WOMAN

One of the age-old challenges women have faced is how much help to expect from other women. Although we found a significant number of women who said they'd had negative or mediocre experiences with female supervisors or colleagues, overall we see leadership and funding circles—by and for female innovators—reshaping the game.

There's a trend of women reaching out to build new networks, organizations, and systems for women to assist each other. Women in the fields of STEM have used both formal and informal systems to support each other in their careers, entrepreneurship, and educational goals. But how far women's networking can go in helping to change the game is yet to come.

Technology has become not only a discipline and a job field, but a dream that draws talent toward it. Shaherose Charania was born in Canada and studied business and technology at the University of Western Ontario. In 2005, she took a leap of faith that would change her life. A friend sold her on the idea of going to Silicon Valley. She had a job interview…but didn't get the job. Nonetheless, she was so entranced with the energy and vision there that she went to her bank, took out a line of credit, and moved to technology's Promised Land, the place where Google was growing and Facebook was taking off.

But things weren't quite what Charania expected. "I arrived here and noticed—it's weird, but I was the only girl in the room. I started to get to know a lot of investors, and they were funding their friends from college, their guy friends from their dorm rooms." At the same time, she was watching female entrepreneurs in emerging economies become more educated and sophisticated and gain access to capital through microloans. As they were continuing to grow in power and develop bigger businesses, the role of women was truly changing in these markets, but "they wouldn't find role models when they looked to the West. Which led to the start of Women 2.0."

Today, Women 2.0 has served hundreds of thousands of people drawn to its community-created content online as well as its conferences and global community for women innovators (all of their programs are open to men as well). Their mission, as stated, "is to increase the number of female founders, employees, and investors in technology startups with inspiration, education, and connections through our platform." The project was born of a mix of serendipity and confusion.

"A friend of mine was working at Facebook (before I could even get an account!) and hosting networking events for young entrepreneurs," said Charania. "Again, I was the only girl. At the third [gathering], he said, 'I know these two other girls I went to college with who are really into tech. They want to start a company; you should meet,' and I was like, 'Really? You wanted us to meet because we're girls?'"

And that's exactly how Women 2.0 was launched. Charania also runs Founder Labs, a five-week program for people with new mobile development projects. For years, she ran Women 2.0 as a side project while working full-time as a project manager and designer and later with Founder Labs. In late 2011, the Kauffman Foundation became a major funder, which allowed Charania to devote the majority of her time to Women 2.0.

For women in tech and innovation, "change has already been more than incremental. We've seen a rise in the number of people coming to our events around the world," and a rise in women seeking to become founders or players in key industries. She credits the rise, in part, to the star status of technologists and business leaders like Mark Zuckerberg and Sheryl Sandberg, who have become household names. Also, building new products does not require deep technical knowledge anymore, especially if it's consumer-driven.

"You can learn the code yourself at coding camps. We're seeing men and women who didn't have those skills take that leap and join something new," she said. "And the quality of the startups we see, it's gone up. I would say in the first one, two, or three years, even, I was like, 'Oh, man, this is a women-led startup, they don't think big enough.' But now they're on par. If you look at our competitions, companies get funding or acquired. There's a track record. To see the change in quality to be totally equivalent to what you'd see at a TechCrunch Disrupt is very indicative of the future of women's roles in innovation."

There are a variety of ways that women give back to other women. Some, like Charania, start networking organizations; others, including venture capitalist Heidi Roizen, mentor informally. Roizen also teaches at Stanford University, a nexus of tech entrepreneurship, bringing women into an inner circle of future business leaders.

Heidi Roizen traces the gender disparities in venture funding to an earlier point in life: education. "Most Silicon Valley technology venture-funded private companies are founded by engineers, and women have a disproportionately small representation in the people coming out of college with degrees in engineering and computer science. I believe ten years from now we're going to see a big change, but that takes all of us continuing to push and continuing to encourage women. For example, I teach entrepreneurship classes at Stanford in the engineering department, and I literally recruit and encourage women to come to my classes. My classes are often oversubscribed, and as the instructor, I get to have a big say on who gets in: For the good of the individuals as well as the quality of the class (which is a discussion class), I tip the scale to try to admit as many women as I can. In a class of fifty, I've had as low as nine, even though I let all female applicants in. But recently, I had so many women on the list I actually had to turn some away or I would have exceeded fifty out of fifty." She also lectures in her class about life-work balance, something she feels the men appreciate as well as the women. Roizen believes that established networks are only one part of the picture.

"This morning, a reporter e-mailed me and asked, 'What women's groups are you a part of? What are the big campaigns and other initiatives that you're leading or advocating?' The truth is I'm not really participating in a lot of formal groups and initiatives. For me, I prefer to use my position, knowledge, and available time to do things more at the individual entrepreneur level. I believe if everybody in positions like mine (male and female, by the way) did more individual ad hoc efforts, we would change the world. For example, I just finished spending a half hour with a female entrepreneur giving her advice. This is not a company that would fit DFJ's investment criteria, and she was not a Stanford student—I just did it to be helpful to a woman entrepreneur, give her a little extra edge." Heidi allocates time nearly every day—often during walks near her home—to meet with entrepreneurs, especially female entrepreneurs, hear their stories, and offer advice.

Kimberly Bryant, an engineer who worked at companies including DuPont and Genentech, takes a different approach—running coding classes for girls, often from poor or working-class neighborhoods. "When I started Black Girls Code in 2011, there weren't any programs that had a foundation in communities of color to teach our kids about technology," said Bryant, the mother of a young daughter. "So our focus is really to drive this whole conversation around why it's important for our kids—both girls and boys—to know how to be creative with technology and not just be delegated to being forever just users and consumers of it. It fosters that conversation not only with the youth, but also within their communities, with their parents, and within their schools."

There are many computer summer camps and enrichment programs available to teens these days—including ones targeting girls, but some of these teen tech camps can cost up to $1,000 per week. Black Girls Code, which is funded partly by foundations, can charge as little as $150 for a six-week session.

Among the contributors in our forum we found robust discussions of the different ways women can help each other in this field, the value of male mentors, and even some critiques of whether women are supportive enough of each other in the field. Megan Groves, a digital marketing consultant and startup mentor said, "I've had a long list of mentors over the years myself—in academia, business, and for general life guidance—and most have been men. Several live in different cities, but we've kept in touch with regular Skype calls and in-person meetings when we find ourselves in the same area. I've seen that many men have a genuine interest in helping bring out the best in the women around them, even when other women may or may not share that desire. I think it's important to seek out women to trust and learn from, but I also believe in accepting support where we can find it."

Yinka Abdu, founder of the online fashion platform Suede Lane, said, "Along with many others, I've found that women are not necessarily supportive of each other in the workplace. I've also found that in the same way that some people like the concept of humanity more than the reality of actually helping humans, some women only pay lip service to the issue of mentorship. They may proclaim (even publicly) to want to help others, yet approaching them or trying to follow up after meeting leads to a dead end. Sad because more female mentorship (especially earlier in one's career, before getting better at spotting B.S.) would help reduce the frequency of incidences where some men don't take you seriously, or their offers of help have ulterior motives, like hitting on you."

Susan Baxter, the executive director of the California State University Program for Education and Research in Biotechnology, was mentored by men while she worked in private industry. "But in the academic part of my career path, a group of us women faculty started having lunch together once a month as our tenure decisions loomed ever closer. Actually, I think 80 percent of the junior women faculty at the institution met for these lunches; there were no tenured women at our location. We became close friends, politically savvy, and quite brave and empowered. I think we all look back on those lunches as important to all of us gaining tenure."

Saru Mahajan, a manager at Sapient Nitro, found that some

of the formal women's interest groups provided community, but not leverage. "I felt they did not provide the critical 'resources' for women to move to the next step. By resources, I mean introductions to key people in the industry, support for promotions, ideas to gain capital investment, etc." Nonetheless, she still found the emotional bonding useful.

In other cases, though, women mentors have crucially changed their protégé's careers. Feben Yohannes, the cofounder of GlobalStudent Social, relates the story of what happened as she sought to reboot her career after moving to the United States.

"During my early stage of redefining my life in the United States, I applied for a position at a company that I knew I was overqualified for and yet had a really hard time even getting an interview. Finally, I reached out to this phenomenal senior executive who, as a woman and a mother, instantly connected with me and made it a mission to get me to an interview process. A chance was all I needed to prove my abilities, and less than a year into that job, I was one of ten receiving an award from a pool of 1,200. Sometimes just a slight crack of the door is all that we need to bust through and show our worth, and if we can multiply that gesture for a few folds, then the ripple effect will be significant."

For Phaedra Pardue, cloud and content consultant at Sohonet Media Network, community can take many forms—from real-life friendships to the circle of contributors we gathered for this book.

"My work colleagues have, in many cases, turned into some of my best friends: Sylvia Oglesbee, Susan Rossi, and Carmen Campbell are all exceptionally accomplished women that have succeeded even when they were dealt a difficult hand. I could not have made it as far as I have without their wisdom, advice, logic, passion, and expertise," she said. "We have organized ways to celebrate and bring women together with women's wisdom dinner parties, where we each lean in and share our collective stories, much like we are doing here in this forum of the Innovating Women project. My favorite mentor is my mother-in-law, Madalene Simons, who was one of the first female stockbrokers (the financial industry is another notoriously male-dominated business). While she always looks picture-perfect in her lovely suits and petite frame, she packs a powerful presence that was undeniably a game changer in her industry. In fact, I knew her long before I ever met my husband, as we both belonged to Portlandia, a women's networking group for female business executives in Portland, Oregon. If I could give any advice to those starting their career, find a group of like-minded people to connect with. It has made all the difference for me."

That Special Place in Hell

LYNN TILTON

Lynn Tilton is the founder and CEO of Patriarch Partners LLC, a holding company with investments in more than seventy-five companies across fourteen industry sectors. Ms. Tilton is passionate about saving American jobs by saving American companies. Since 2000, through affiliated investment funds, Tilton has had ownership in and restructured more than 240 companies with combined revenues in excess of $100 billion, representing more than 675,000 jobs. Tilton's platform is the largest woman-owned business in the country.

Our journeys, as women of industry, technology, or service—are lonely and fraught with obstacles unknown to men. We face a choice and consequent juggling act indigenous to our sex—the election whether or not to bear children and, if so selected, the split-of-self required to rear our young without losing the propensity of trajectory to our career paths.

This unrivaled quest to "have it all," to "excel at both," or the unbearable compromise to "sacrifice one for the other" should bind us and unite us in the awe and appreciation of modern womanhood. But instead, few of us find the support system, the sponsors, or the advocates to drive us forward when the darkness envelops us and the battles overwhelm us.

It need not be this way. It should not be lonely, but the path lively with the laughter and love of female friendship. I have often stated in speech and written word that our destinies, as women, will change when we begin by being kind to each other. We can then expect men to take their cue from us. But rather than blame exogenous forces or the male population, we should begin with that which we can control: our own behaviors. Madeline Albright is well-known for her myriad achievements and her celebrated statement, the often-repeated but little practiced, "there is a special place in hell for women who are unkind to women." If this is, indeed, so, then there will be far too many of us in this reserved station. Why do we compete with and cannibalize each other rather than support and promote? Why do we little understand that we are 52 percent of the population and we need not be rivals for a few token places at the top of our profession, but rather, together, we can open access to many more doors?

We live in a country where we can embrace every liberty, gain admission to every institution of higher education, and find entry into every professional field. We, as women, graduate at the top of our classes in undergraduate, legal, business, STEM, and medical educations. And yet, when we look to the top echelons of our respective fields, so few of us sit at the top. This truth must give us pause, force self-reflection, and make us ask: "Why?"

When does our natural predilection to compete against, cannibalize, or deprecate each other begin? What is the invisible force that separates us, rather than binds us, as we grow from young girls and students into womanhood? Are we inculcated to believe that there is only one man for every woman, that a soul mate must be unearthed and protected, and that we must contend like gladiators in the coliseum to war for the prize? Are we unable to relinquish that battle mentality of all is fair in love and war when we enter arenas apart from the heart?

If for no other reason than to honor those unable to embrace freedoms of rights, education, and career, we must consciously connect in their name; we must put envy and competition in its proper place. In messages sent to me, two dear friends, devoted to women less fortunate, reminded me that the liberties that fuel our infinite potential are not accessible to all our global sisters. In Iran, women battle bravely to reclaim the freedoms granted when Shah Pahlavi desegregated the genders in his modernization of democratic Iran. In a campaign called My Stealthy Freedom, courageous women work to retake, by might, these freedoms lost in the Islamic revolution. They long for the power and support of a global sisterhood, a concept that seems unlikely to me until we find power and poetry in force on our western shores.

Of one inalienable truth I am certain: together, standing shoulder to shoulder, women are the greatest force of nature. I also know that when we cease to dilute our power in the name of politics, religion, and male attention, we will be introduced to the best version of collective self. The Dalai Lama has opined that women will be the salvation of the world in the communal power of their compassion. And compassion is contagious.

I struggle to find the voice or the tool that can convince us that we can be strengthened in force by the power of our passion, the depth of our creativity, and the concentration of our collective compassion. I know I have found my harshest critics in other women. Press articles most deeply critical of my style of appearance and leadership were written by women. The harshest of legal scrutiny has been initiated by women. Do we somehow think that we score extra points if we hurt one of our own? It is not that those in their professions should not be critical of women if it is so deserved. However, it seems most often that women, in their quest for approval and career advancement, often find force in preying on their own, as if they are in some way weaker and easier game in the hunt.

As a single mother at twenty-three, I have known the fear of being lost in the darkness, the uncertainty of finding my way into the light. There were many days when I was just unsure I could survive the burden to keep my daughter safe and my job secure. We are all shaped by our experiences and our reactions to our tragedies, and triumphs profile who we will become. I know I want the journey to be easier for my daughter and her daughters. I appreciate also that I must not just utter this prayer of hope, but I must be a crusader of change and an example of the expectation I establish.

I have built a business where each day I attempt to prove that making money and making the world a better place are not mutually exclusive goals. I do this by buying companies that others have left to liquidate and by seeking to rebuild, rejuvenate, and reinvent. By doing so, I hope to protect those working at these businesses from the indignity of returning home to their families without work.

As technology advances with exponential speed and jobs are replaced by automation, artificial intelligence, and robotics, I strive to bridge technology with humanity and manufacturing with innovation. All things begin with product—design and disruption—and I struggle to dream, design, build, and create the 360 experiences with sufficient speed to keep these companies, many centennial and iconic, relevant and alive.

My dream is to end the plague of joblessness. But my new hope is to inspire women to unearth their collective strength, deeply rooted in female creativity and compassion, so that we might find a way to unite on our journeys. We can be smart, sexy, and sophisticated and still rule the world.

Perhaps this evolution must start with young girls before they grow jaded. I have reintroduced an old cosmetic brand—Jane Cosmetics—for younger women, where for every cosmetic item that is purchased, the company gives one to a shelter for battered women in your community—"buy one, give one to a neighbor in need." It is my confidence that through this company we can help teach a younger generation of women that compassion is contagious and that kindness can be the new cool. I have dedicated my efforts and my companies' sponsorship to support Dean Kamen in his FIRST robotics competition in order to attract a larger populace of girls by making certain they never feel the need to choose between brains and beauty. I am in the process of posting the X Prize that I have designed and funded, which will offer an extra $5 million to any winning X Prize team that boasts a female CEO and women in half its leadership roles. Perhaps the size of the prize will inspire the drafting of brilliant women to the technology teams advancing solutions to the world's largest problems.

I hope that one day soon I can call upon the women I know, and those I hope to know, so that we might select an audacious and measurable goal, where efforts, by women for women, will be set and achieved. I remain convinced that we will unite in thought and action when we can prove to each other that our power lies in numbers, and quantify the improvement in our lives that is demonstrated when we stand in support and show kindness to each other. Let us be each other's cheerleader, friend, and the invisible web of energetic elegance that transcends dream to reality and drives our reach for the stars.

The Virtuous Circle

Women-owned businesses show great promise, even outperforming male-owned ones. For example, women-owned businesses with more than $10 million in revenue have a growth rate 47 percent greater than all companies with revenue of $10 million and up. In the decade between 2002 to 2012, women-owned businesses have grown 28.6 percent relative to 24.4 percent increase in all business.[17] According to the Center for Women's Business Research, 41 percent of private companies in the United States are owned by women, but only 3 to 5 percent of them get venture funding.[18] An entire cadre of organizations has risen to meet the need of evaluating women-led firms for funding and making sure they get what they deserve. Some, like Astia and Double Digit Academy, offer training; others, including Springboard and 37 Angels, focus on funding. Golden Seeds, founded in 2004, is a membership-based investor group, founded initially by women on Wall Street, which funds women-led firms. Its membership today is 80 percent women.

Businesswoman Loretta McCarthy is the co-chair of the New York chapter of Golden Seeds—its largest. After two-plus combined decades of working as a senior level marketing executive at American Express and then Oppenheimer Funds, she said, "I really learned a huge amount about networking. Obviously much of my knowledge is about marketing, but I also learned a great deal about money management and the capital markets. Here at Golden Seeds, I'm able to combine a

---

[17] "Growing Under the Radar: An Exploration of the Achievements of Million-Dollar Women-Owned Firms," American Express OPEN, January 2013.

[18] Jessica Bruder, "We Need More Female Venture Capitalists," June 30, 2010.

great deal of that because we think about how to build great companies. A lot of that is marketing, so I can bring that skill to these companies."

McCarthy added that during her years at those companies, "I picked up a comfort level with talking about the capital markets so that facing an investment decision for these companies is not daunting to me. And when you're running a membership organization, which is really what this is, you spend a great deal of time thinking about how you create an environment that will make members satisfied to be here, eager to participate, willing to write checks to invest in companies, and inclined to renew year after year after year so that you build a large group of members who are doing this important work."

Today, Golden Seeds has more than 300 members, all of whom are investors. As she points out, women start half of the companies launched in America. "But in 2005, they were getting less than 5 percent of the capital that was being invested in new businesses. There were very few big businesses, publicly-held companies, or large growth categories like Google that were started by women. The other part of the equation was that in 2004, when we first were conceiving Golden Seeds, women were only 5 percent of the Americans who were participating in angel investing." In 2012, that number reached 21 percent.[19]

Successes like this have emboldened Golden Seeds, as has the strength of the companies it has chosen to work with. McCarthy said, "We try to be as active as we can be. We currently have forty-eight companies in our portfolio. Three companies have had good exits. Five have wound down. That's a pretty good rate." Usually a member of Golden Seeds takes a seat on the board, which, given the organization's overwhelmingly female membership, often added to board diversity.

"We nearly always have one of our members occupy a board seat," said McCarthy. "Frequently, when the companies come to us, it is the first time they created the board of directors, so it is the first time the company has had to cope with having outside

[19] Jeffrey Sohl, "The Angel Investor Market in 2012: A Moderating Recovery Continues," Center for Venture Research, April 25, 2013.

people suddenly sitting at the table and giving them advice. But we also spend a fair amount of time with all companies, thinking about how we can be helpful outside of that one board representative, how we can be helpful to the company at various stages of the company's growth. One of the most valuable assets at Golden Seeds are those 300 people who are our members, who have had long careers, and frequently are very connected. We have a lot of financial people here, but we also have marketing, social media, technology, and other expertise that we can call in even on a short time frame to help." In other words, whether we are talking about networking, mentoring, education, or finance, the world's virtuous circle of innovating women are stepping up to help each other.

CHAPTER 3
EDUCATE TO INNOVATE

Not everyone has, in those awkward teen and tween years, the composure of Emily Fowler. She's now cofounder and VP of Possibilities at HeroX, an innovation group that encourages competition to solve big problems and grew from the X Prize model. "When I was in tenth grade, my dad found out about this summer camp called 'Get Wired Get Hired,' which was held at Bentley University. My dad was a stockbroker professionally, but a computer nerd passionately. As such, he always taught me about computers as he built and programmed them. He found out about this program and recommended that I go. I thought it sounded really cool—it was a computer camp for girls. How fun!" She continues, "I've never been one to be self-conscious about being cool or uncool. Seriously, thank gosh for that—my parents (and teachers) instilled a strong sense of self. When I chose to attend the camp, I was teased by kids from school upon my return. It didn't help that the local newspaper had featured a story about me attending the camp—they were trying to highlight and encourage more girls to attend tech-oriented camps."

When the high school crowd tried to tear her down, Emily wasn't buying it. "The stereotypes were your traditional comments like 'nerd,' 'dork,' 'loser.' Oh, and my personal favorite was 'lesbian.' Fortunately, I didn't care, and I had a sharp enough mouth at a young age that when people—and by people, I do mean guys—said that to me, I would just retort with, 'First of all, being a lesbian is not an insult. Secondly, being smart or curious doesn't make me a lesbian. What did you learn at football camp?' Girls teased me as well, and that was a bit hurtful. Mostly, they were concerned that I would be seen as a lesbian. Again, I didn't care—I wasn't interested in impressing a guy who didn't think I was cool just the way I was. I knew from a young age that I wanted to attract people who were like me."

Now Emily's job includes taking what she learned while working as a director at the X Prize and applying it to new enterprises. She credits her father with inspiration. "My dad's influence was mainly in his encouragement of my involvement with computers," she said. "He just made it seem so fun and exclusive—like I was learning how to do something that only adults knew how to do."

"Education" can cover a lot of ground when it comes to women learning science, math, technology, engineering, and business. There are the early years, when parental, scholastic, and societal factors can encourage or discourage girls. Then, as Emily Fowler found, there are the teen and tween years—middle/junior high school through high school in the United States. Teasing and judgments can be merciless. College presents a different set of challenges, with professors not always able to see equal potential in different genders and races. And finally, there is adult education—whether it comes in the form of signing up for a MOOC (a massive open online course you follow on your computer—some free, some for a fee, some for degree credit) or short-term intensives like Hacker School.

And of course, it's worth remembering that before educational biases and discrepancies come cultural biases carried from generation to generation. Sunny Bates is the CEO of Red Thread, which works with the threads and people that shape the future. She is a founding board member of Kickstarter and Creative Capital and is on the TED brain trust. She shares a conversation she had with a new mother: "When she had a girl, everyone was, 'Oh she's so pretty, she's so beautiful,' and all these dresses came. Then when she had a boy, it was all about the San Francisco Giants and the future president of the United States. No one once said, 'Oh he's beautiful.' No one once said, 'Here's your daughter, the future president of the United States.' That's where we go [mentally], and our society carries those presumptions forward as our kids grow." Gender issues can also get lost in translation, metaphorically speaking. A study on immigrant girls growing up in the United States found that they thought women could not become president because of a classroom poster depicting all male presidents.[20]

How girls and women enter—and, unfortunately, often exit—the STEM education pipeline is the crux of the problem. There's a need to increase their numbers and perseverance and strengthen all levels of STEM education for women and girls. In 2010, the Bayer Corporation ran a survey that found 40 percent of women and minority chemists and chemical engineers had been discouraged from pursuing their field, most often by college professors. The survey respondents identified three top factors that helped keep women and minorities from majoring in STEM: lack of quality science and math education programs in poorer school districts (75 percent), persistent stereotypes that say STEM isn't for girls or minorities (66 percent), and financial issues related to the cost of education (53 percent).[21]

So how do innovating women get their start? Their introductions to the fields of business and STEM reflect a wide range of responses to girls who are curious and interested in pursuing knowledge normally thought of as "a boy thing" or "a man thing."

Kristen Sanderson, consulting engineer at GE Energy Managements, said, "I have to credit my father for encouraging me early on. He always told me I could do anything without boundaries or restrictions. I don't want to leave out my mom, who also encouraged me to become a professional. She went back to school and earned her accounting degree and went on to be a banker and CEO of our family construction business." During high school, her father encouraged her to study

[20] Lee L, "Understanding Gender Through Disney's Marriages: A Study of Young Korean Immigrant Girls," *Early Childhood Education Journal* [serial online]. August 2008;36(1):11-18. Available from: Education Full Text (H.W. Wilson), Ipswich, MA.

[21] "Bayer Facts of Science Education XIV: Female and Minority Chemists and Chemical Engineers Speak About Diversity and Underrepresentation in STEM," Executive Summary, Bayer Corporation, March 2010, 15, 21.

computing. "I went to my university at registration and changed my major from pre-business to pre-engineering. I received my degree in computer science and went on to work on software system control centers for utility companies."

Pam Barry is the cofounder and COO of the digital media and branding company Customerforce.com. She recalls, "My father suggested I had the aptitude to be a computer programmer. I was told by my career guidance counselor that I would be lucky if I could get a job as a computer operator, never mind programmer. My mother was furious with her, and my parents set out to help prove her wrong. At age seventeen, I took two aptitude tests for two different organizations and was offered a position with both as a programmer. Chose one of the offers and dropped my applications for university."

And Evonne Heyning found herself caught in a squeeze play between parental support and inadequate educational resources in her district. Still, as a young girl, she helped change the system. "When we go to school for the first time, we start to differentiate ourselves from the others. We figure out that we are better at some things than others, and we form our identities and often our livelihoods based on those early ideas," she said. "Early childhood was fantastic—it felt like a playground of possibilities. My dad would buy me tests to do, and I was reading the newspaper long before starting school with a fantastic first-year teacher in kindergarten. She fought for my right to compete and win math competitions and winked at me in the hallway when she saw me frowning. I started programming computers at the age of six, in 1981. My school had no idea what to do with a precocious prodigy who was learning algebra, exhibiting modernist art downtown, and asking for more work to do. My frustrated teacher sent me to the library, where they put me in front of the one computer they had in the school and gave me the spiral-bound book of BASIC. Heaven is no class and programming all afternoon!"

Heyning continues, "I enjoyed math, art, and natural hands-on learning opportunities and began to create books, games, and programs to share with teachers, counselors, and the principal. They took me to the state capitol building in Richmond, Virginia, and before my seventh birthday, I lobbied the state to put computers in every school. We won. At eight, I was asked to leave public school because they did not have any more resources to give me until middle school. As a geeky white girl growing up as a minority in the city, my parents were afraid what would happen if I skipped ahead again, so they found a scholarship for a private school where there were more resources for exploring my creative potential." Heyning is now a cofounder at EDDEFY, which produces online tools for lifelong learning.

And Fiona Nielsen, the founder and CEO at DNAdigest. org, a nonprofit organization promoting and enabling mechanisms for efficient and secure sharing of genomics data for research, said that her early years were also a time of accelerated learning, but not through schools. "My introduction to the technical side of STEM came from my grandfather. He would tell me a lot about a lot of things, including archaeology and history, but he really caught my interest when he put me on his lap and showed me how he could type in the BASIC code from a computer magazine and turn it into a live game on his computer," she said. "My grandfather was also the first person I know to have a personal website. He proudly showed me his website, hosted by some company in the United States because back then there were no Internet hosting companies in Denmark. Thanks to him, I was curious about the Internet, and I taught myself HTML and JavaScript from books I borrowed from the library to launch my own homepage back in 1996. In summary, all my main inspirations have come from outside of school and especially from 'real world' applications and from inspirational people."

Natalie Panek, mission systems engineer at MDA Robotics and Automation, which produces Canadian robotics and other hardware for space exploration programs, feels that utilizing today's social communication tools can help fight the stereotypes and peer pressure that keeps some girls from math and science. "Media is such a huge part of Gen Y—almost everything youth consumes is through their phones, Internet like YouTube, or television. We need to be providing access to amazing female role models through streams youth actually use. The Twitter world and other forms of social media are generally inundated with many hardships and challenges women in technology face. This negative perspective will not help inspire the next generation." Panek spoke at TedxYouthToronto, demonstrating her love for the field. She added, "It's like going on a first date; I'm not going to tell you all of my flaws right away. I am going to impress you with my most desirable traits first! So we must inspire and motivate first, then help build the skills women need to succeed and excel in the fields of STEM."

Educational tracking can also be a bane to girls studying math and science. Xerox Chief Technology Officer Sophie Vandebroek shares her shock at finding out that at her daughter's school, only one girl was put in the advanced math program, while her daughter and her friends were put in the regular level despite their achievements: "I called the other moms and we complained and then they put the girls back in advanced math. So even schools unconsciously put the girls into less scientific fields, and once you do that in the middle school, you lose them. So you have to really be on top of them. It was the same girls that got into advanced math in middle school that then ended up all getting into science, three of them engineers and the fourth one is now in medical school."

Disrupting My Way Through Life

DEBORAH MILLS-SCOFIELD

Deborah Mills-Scofield is a strategy and innovation consultant to mid/large corporations and partner in Glengary LLC, an early-stage venture capital firm. She's also a visiting scholar, mentor, and advisor at Brown University. Her patent from AT&T Bell Labs was one of the highest revenue-generating patents for AT&T and Lucent.

In order to more wisely mentor young entrepreneurs and college kids, I've been reflecting on my own personal and professional life. It seems disruption has been an unplanned, unconscious, and common theme.

Disruption started early, when my parents didn't let me go to school five days a week for fear I'd become average. My mom took me into New York City to go to museums most Tuesdays, when the museums were free, and on Fridays, we'd frequently go in the city just to experience it. Needless to say, my public school teachers were thoroughly frustrated with my parents—although they couldn't complain about my grades.

At Brown University, disruption was the status quo, so I felt right at home. Three of us young women helped start the Cognitive Science program there, one of the first at the undergraduate level. Our dean and professors helped us create this brand-new concentration, and we women were the first to graduate with the degree! Looking back, I realize it was my first entrepreneurial activity, although I didn't know it at the time.

I graduated from Brown in three years at the age of twenty and went to Bell Labs to work as the systems engineer for AT&T's messaging systems. While there, I thought: instead of designing separate architectures, wouldn't it just be easier to have one that handled different types of media according to technical capabilities? So that's what I did. Although I couldn't legally drink or rent a car, I did get a patent for this innovation, which later became one of AT&T/Lucent's highest revenue-generating patents. Simultaneously, my boss successfully made the case for me to be a Member of Technical Staff without the requisite PhD. Throughout my entire career, I defined and redefined what I did and how I did it, including internal startups (and startdowns), the Bell Labs way.

When my fiancé left basic research at Bell Labs to teach physics at Oberlin College, my Bell Labs director worked with his AT&T counterpart to move me to Cleveland as well so that I wouldn't quit. They set me up with a fabulous home office and flew me to my New Jersey office or elsewhere in the world every week. My management recognized my talent and was determined to use our technology as advertised and not to let distance get in the way! Nine years later, when I had my children and refused to travel, they made all sorts of accommodations so that I wouldn't quit. Having management that not only recognized my value, but also used personal capital to keep me, was disruptive.

When I finally quit AT&T, I didn't know anyone in Cleveland. I had two children, was the main breadwinner, and wasn't sure what I'd do. I reached out to Brown's Northeast Ohio Alumni network, and everything evolved from there—I found the clients for my consulting business and started my partnership, as the only woman, in an early-stage venture capital firm. My husband's willingness to be a full partner in raising our children and managing a home has made these serial disruptions possible.

A wonderful benefit of being disruptive is that I get to pass it on—my greatest achievements are all wrapped up in people.

My relationships with and mentoring of entrepreneurs and students, especially at Brown, will hopefully have a long-lasting impact—beyond even the impressive work they do for kids with cancer, teaching different languages, taking medical equipment to Zanzibar, and helping inner-city middle school kids learn to love math, just to name a few. My work with the engineering, science, art, and design schools and departments at Brown will enable more learning by doing and more experimenting–learning–applying–iterating, which can make a faster positive impact on society.

Mostly, though, I hope that my children will look at me and see what is possible, how they can make a difference and shape the world, how they can disrupt the status quo and also give back along the way. My guiding principle has always been that at the end of the day, the only thing that matters is that I can look myself in the mirror—that my integrity and character cannot be compromised. Fortunately I've been surrounded throughout my life by family, friends, and management who have supported and upheld those same values. Who knows what I will be doing a few years from now? Maybe this, and maybe something else, but I can promise it will be disruptive.

How I Kept Going

ANASILVIA SALAZAR,
TRANSLATED BY CECILIA CASTILLO

Anasilvia Salazar was born in San Antonio Huista, Huehuetenango, Guatemala and is a lifelong technology lover. Thanks to a grant from the Juan Bautista Gutierrez Foundation she was able to study Engineering and Computer Science at the Universidad del Valle de Guatemala, graduating cum laude in 2013. She currently works as an Analyst in MultiInvestment Corporation.

Cecilia Castillo is a software engineer with postgraduate studies in network and information security. She is a tech lover and athlete who works as CTO in Elementalgeeks, based in Guatemala. She promotes the participation of women in the technology area and teaching high school students about electronics (girlsattech.org). Anasilvia Salazar is a student of engineering in computer science.

As a little girl in San Antonia Huista, a small town in Guatemala, I was very interested in anything involving technology. Although we didn't have a lot of electronics in my home, that didn't stop my curiosity. I remember, when I was about twelve, how much I loved to visit my cousins—my uncle, working in the United States, sent my cousins a laptop exclusively for games, and my cousins let me borrow it anytime I wanted.

I enjoyed disassembling watches, lamps, remote controls—anything that belonged to me or that nobody was using anymore. My grandpa repaired electronic equipment and taught me my first lessons about electronics in his workshop. After I took something apart, I'd try to make something new with the pieces. It was always a great achievement to finally make something work.

When I was eleven, my godparents paid for my first months of computer classes at the only computer academy in town. The school wasn't very good, but I learned to use Word, Excel, and PowerPoint. I enrolled in high school in order to teach (a high school education is a requirement for obtaining a teaching certificate in Guatemala) and took classes in computer studies there, too, but I didn't learn much of anything new there—only how to make macros in Excel.

I was fifteen when my mom bought me my first computer. It was a secondhand Dell with a Pentium® III processor and no more than 40GB of hard drive and 512MB of RAM. It was white with a horizontal case. It was slow, but I loved it.

In 2008, I graduated from high school with many honors, including a certificate to be an elementary school teacher—but I still had many dreams. I decided instead of teaching I wanted to study engineering and focus on computers, and I wanted to go to one of the best universities in the country: Universidad del Valle de Guatemala. It was still just a dream, but a dream that I knew I had to make come true.

I managed to do it with three things: determination, pursuance, and perseverance. I applied to the scholarship program sponsored by the Fundación Juan Bautista Gutiérrez, which gives six scholarships annually to talented students with few resources to continue their university studies. The process wasn't easy: it went through many stages, including skill evaluations, psychological tests, interviews, and socioeconomic studies. I am a committed Catholic, and my life revolves around God, so there wasn't a single day when I didn't pray for one of the scholarships—and I got one. By the end of that year, I knew I would be studying engineering and computers at the Universidad del Valle de Guatemala the following fall.

I was very nervous and a little scared when I first went to college. I was scared because I knew very little calculus, physics, and chemistry, and absolutely no programming. Adapting was very difficult that first semester. I was in an unknown city, far from family and friends, and facing a career that would be a challenge for anyone with even average expectations. But to keep the scholarship, my average GPA had to stay at or above a 3.5—which concerned me a lot, because in the beginning my grades were pretty bad.

In Guatemala, the college environment for women in tech is extremely challenging since most of the students are men, and more generally, women are relegated to the background in our society. On many occasions, I had to hold back tears while listening to sexist remarks from my male classmates. I grew up in a home with good values, firmly grounded in respect, so it was hard to hear comments that insulted the dignity of women and questioned their ability to succeed in a career that, according to many, was meant only for men.

Studying at the university became more and more intolerable every day, and eventually, along with a friend in the program who was experiencing the same thing, I decided to report the situation to a campus counselor, who put us in touch with a support group. Our relationships with our classmates began to improve, but I can't remember any semester in which I didn't suffer—studying all night, giving up my social life, and constant stress and sacrifices. Every year, the subjects became harder, but I conquered each one of them—except Compilers I and Compilers II. Compilers was my Achilles' heel. I really thought that was the end of my career in tech. First I couldn't program my own parser, and in Compilers II, I couldn't program my own compiler. I really believed that I had failed and would lose the scholarship, but thank God, I had a brilliant teacher who was very patient with me. Without him, I couldn't have possibly passed these classes; and even though I passed with the minimum score, I learned more than I ever imagined I would.

In February 2012, I applied for another scholarship, sponsored by Gulf Business Machines, or GBM, an IBM Alliance Company and a well-known technology entity in Guatemala. Its scholarship program gives outstanding students an opportunity to be offered a job at GBM after spending a year learning a specialty in one of its departments. The selection process was long, but I was chosen for a scholarship, which launched my first experience in the working world.

Now I am in my last semester at university, poised to graduate at the end of this year, and there is nothing more gratifying than seeing myself succeed against all expectations. I will never forget the words that I heard from a classmate when I first went to college: *"She won't finish the first year. In 'Compu,' only a few survive. She's a woman, and she comes from a small country town."* Those words left a mark on me. How was it possible in the twenty-first century that people would still harbor this kind of prejudice? But that's the reality in which we live.

I hope many women will begin to enter careers in science, engineering, electronics, mathematics, and technology, which are traditionally labeled for men. My story is proof that women from anywhere with any sort of background can prevail.

Getting to the Ivory Tower

Many things have changed between the time when Kimberly Bryant was a student and the time in which her daughter is growing up. Technology is now ubiquitous. But teens in high school or college often face a double whammy of peer pressure and the weeding out process that happens in challenging majors or majors where the pool of class availability is restricted. Culture can deepen the divide. In the lead to a 2011 *New Yorker* article titled, "Can Sheryl Sandberg Upend Silicon Valley's Male-Dominated Cult," Ken Auletta writes, "Several female computer science majors at Stanford pointed to the depiction of women in films like *The Social Network*, where the boys code and the girls dance around in their underwear."[22] From media to peers to academic preparation, a variety of factors can shape how well young women fare in the fields of STEM.

Priyanka Pathak began as an international business major at the University of Texas at Austin. She decided to take a few programming classes and then made choices based both on academics and on her peer group. "I had always been naturally good at languages, and when I thought about computers as machines, whose language you had to learn to speak, it felt more doable. I also took an introductory computer science [CS] course for nonmajors at the urging of my advisor and sailed right through it—in fact, the CS department chair pulled me aside and offered me a full scholarship if I decided to pursue computer science as a major instead. Knowing perfectly well that it was mostly because I was a girl and they had very few females in their department, and after seeing that I could not relate whatsoever

[22] Ken Auletta, "A Woman's Place: Can Sheryl Sandberg Upend Silicon Valley's male-dominated culture?" *The New York Times*, July 11, 2011.

to any of the few CS girls I met, I turned it down. The reasons: a) I wanted to be a leader, and I believed that CS would never lead to any kind of leadership possibility (but the business school information systems track emphasized that aspect); b) I didn't want to be lonely without like-minded friends, nor did I want to embody the stereotype of a geeky coder; and c) I had never heard of a successful female computer scientist who I felt was outgoing, ambitious, and socially conscious like me. I also wasn't convinced they were offering the scholarship to me on ability alone, and based on my previous experiences, I was secretly afraid I'd be bad at the higher-level math-intensive courses and disappoint everyone. However, partly as a compromise and partly because I had liked my information systems courses and not been challenged enough by the international business coursework, I switched to MIS [Management Information Systems, or how to design and use technology in organizations] as my major and took supplementary computer science coursework." She added, "As a girl, I was always the definite minority in my MIS and CS classes, but I pushed through and had plenty of friends through other classes/organizations to support me. With two friends, I applied my new technical expertise by taking on an ed-tech project based in Panama and later turning it into a separate student organization. The project was even accepted to the Clinton Global Initiative University, for which I now serve as a mentor. Ultimately, all my STEM-related efforts were rewarded when I was accepted to graduate school at Columbia University to pursue my passion: designing, building, and implementing technologies that address issues in global health and international development."

Pathak's story illustrates that even some women and girls who get outside validation still have to push through self-doubt. And not all faculty are supportive. A 2012 Princeton University study titled "Science faculty's subtle gender biases favor male students" stated in its abstract, "In a randomized, double-blind study...science faculty from research-intensive universities rated the application materials of a student—who was randomly assigned either a male or female name—for a laboratory manager position. Faculty participants rated the male applicant as significantly more competent and hirable than the (identical) female applicant. These participants also selected a higher starting salary and offered more career mentoring to the male applicant. The gender of the faculty participants did not affect responses, such that female and male faculty were equally likely to exhibit bias against the female student." In other words, both male and female professors exhibited bias against female students.[23]

For Maria Thompson, global innovation framework facilitator for Illinois Tool Works Solutions, discouragement came a bit earlier. "My high school guidance counselor told me that I should NOT major in computer engineering in college. He said, 'How do you think you are going to come back here and get a job with a degree like that?' No kidding. It was 1978. I was top of class with a 4.0 GPA. I didn't know what to major in, but, of course, I thought I could do anything. I studied the literature, and I intuited that computers were going to change the world, and I wanted to be part of that change. I graduated top of my computer science class four years later and went to Bell Laboratories and then to Motorola, with successful careers at both. I never did go back and apply for a job in my hometown."

There has actually been a reversal of fortune for women in terms of the overall percent of working professionals, a trend that now seems poised to turn around. According to the Bureau of Labor Statistics, from 2000 to 2011, women working in professional computing jobs decreased 8 percent, to 25 percent of the total, while the number of men climbed 16 percent.[24] Historian Janet Abbate is the author of *Recoding Gender: Women's Changing Participation in Computing* and an associate professor at Virginia Tech. She said the percentage of female programmers and scientists has declined since the 1980s. Computing

[23] Corinne A. Moss-Racusina, John F. Dovidio, Victoria L. Brescoll, Mark J. Graham, and Jo Handelsman. "Science Faculty's Subtle Gender Biases Favor Male Students." Proceedings of the National Science Academy of the United States of America. September 17, 2012.

[24] Claire Cain Miller, "In Google's Inner Circle, a Falling Number of Women," *The New York Times*, August 22, 2012.

education, with specialization happening earlier during college years, "is more competitive and a bit more narrow than it used to be. In the sixties and the seventies, there were some computer science programs, but a lot of people added computing [to their studies] from other backgrounds, and that was considered normal. Now it's more of an expectation that you're going to kind of follow the straight line through computer science. This especially applies to women because they often come to their interest in computing later. If you look at a teenaged level, I think gender roles are quite strong, and [computing] seems kind of geeky, and masculine women and those girls don't necessarily want to do it. Then when they're a little bit more mature and in college, they're like, 'I am interested in this,' but then they've already fallen behind." Abbate is also tracking another trend. "Computing is becoming increasingly more interdisciplinary. I think that's good for women because they have a high interest in interdisciplinary work."

So if, as historian Abbate argues, computing and technology become gendered at an early age, what happens to those women who decide a bit later on that they want to be programmers or engineers? One possible solution is to head to an organization that trains early- or mid-career workers to code. Hackbright, an all-female software engineering school, has a partnership, known as the Moms in Tech Sponsorship, with Facebook, which covers the $12,000 tuition cost. The program's goal is to provide mothers, who have left the field to focus on their children and are now returning, with up-to-date coding skills so that they can apply for engineering manager or technical woman leader positions.

The technology company Etsy, which powers sales from individual artisans from around the world, helped sponsor scholarships specifically for women via Hacker School, which offers a three-month program described as "a writer's retreat for hackers." Over the past couple of years, the number of women engineers on Etsy's staff has also grown considerably; by March 2013, it included twenty women out of 110 total. While still only 18 percent of the engineering staff is women, it's considered among the better in the industry. It also represents an effort by the company to recognize that if 80 percent of their customers are women, their engineering team needed more gender diversity[25] (Disclosure: coauthor Farai Chideya briefly worked at Etsy.)

We spoke with Hacker School cofounder Nick Bergson and with Betsy Cannon, who attended Hacker School and now works as a product engineer at Tumblr. For Nick, the purpose is bigger than any individual career. "Right now we have a huge shortage of qualified programmers in this country. Women are half of the world, and right now, very few women are programmers. And so we have this huge potential supply of good programmers. It's a huge problem for us to fix."

Betsy Cannon added, "I would also say that with women—and also with any type of diversity—that you get a new perspective. When you think about the Internet…I work at Tumblr, and a huge percentage of our user base is female. So it makes sense that you have a female perspective and notice what they care about. A lot of the times women come up with really creative solutions, sometimes because they have different backgrounds. I know a female coder whose background is in psychology, and so she's able to think through different steps and see, 'Oh, this is the feeling to this part [of interacting with a piece of technology or a platform] for someone.'"

"When we first started," said Bergson of Hacker School, which he founded with friends David Albert and Sonali Sridhar, "5 percent of our students were women. Today, for our last four batches, between 30 and 45 percent of our students have been women. So we have kind of a controlled experiment, being able to look at how Hacker School felt when there was only 5 percent women, meaning, basically, one or two women in the room, to almost having gender parity. Across the board, we ourselves, and our students, men and women alike, report that they like the environment more now that it is more gender-balanced."

---

[25] Leslie Bradshaw, "Martha Kelly Girdler on How to Cultivate More Female Engineers and on Being Part of Etsy's 500% Success Story," *Forbes*, March 4, 2013.

Hacker School also demands students don't indulge in subtle signals of racism or sexism. "Something we've seen in a lot of the parts of the world is that with sexism, because it can be so subtle, frequently people feel like they have only two options," said Bergson. "The first is to either say nothing, in which case things just kind of build up and simmer over time. The other is to feel like you have to make a big deal out of everything, and then you get this backlash and people aren't comfortable about that. So what we've tried to develop at Hacker School is essentially a third way. We have these lightweight social rules to give people an opportunity to respond to things and say, 'Hey, that made me feel a little bit uncomfortable,' and just address it there, not make a big deal out of it, and not feel like you have to repress it or not say anything. That third way allows people to work together much more comfortably and safely, and therefore makes a much better learning environment. We added that a little over a year ago."

Betsy Cannon went to Hacker School in a class that was about 35 percent women. She compares that to taking computer science in school. "In my advanced algorithms class in college, it was a class of about thirty-five, and there were four women in it, so just over 10 percent. I was in other classes that were about a quarter women, one out of four. [In the classes that were overwhelmingly male] I would actually look around the classroom and could recognize the women, and I would actually count them, whereas in other classes I wouldn't really care what the percentage was. I was like, 'There's enough [women] in general.' And when you realize you've reached such a low point, like around 10 percent, you start thinking of yourself as a minority. So you spend energy thinking about that, rather than focusing on your work. It can get distracting."

Hacker School now partners with women's industry groups like the Ada Initiative and with companies that sponsor grants for women. But one effect of the rising gender parity, said Bergson, was that "it also attracted women who didn't need financial assistance, who decided to apply and didn't request grants. They saw that it [i.e., gender-equality in technology] was something that we really cared about, and that we were making an explicit invitation to women, and that we were putting our money where our mouth was." He emphasizes the school did not "lower the bar at all for women. I think that helps a lot, because then we don't end up with an environment, for instance, where all of the women are beginners, or not as good programmers." The school reports that men seem more satisfied with the better gender mix, too.

CHAPTER 4
WOMEN FOR THE WORLD

Technologies are tools; nothing more, nothing less. They can be used for good or ill and implemented in the context of for-profit companies, nonprofits, or social enterprise hybrids. Many women want to address the thorny technical issues of global importance. They seek not only a return on their investments, but a social return as well—a way to leverage technology and entrepreneurship for a greater good.

Imagine going back to your native country with your husband and new baby to cast one of the most important votes of your life, only to witness an election overtaken by violence and your country spiraling out of control. That was exactly the situation in which Ory Okolloh found herself at the end of December 2007 and the first few weeks of 2008. She transformed that experience into Ushahidi, a website that allows ordinary citizens to collect, record, and crowdsource eyewitness accounts of violence and crisis information using text messages on simple cell phones and Google Maps.

A Kenyan national, Okolloh suddenly found herself caught up in the aftermath when the postelection violence broke out. Because of what she called "self-censorship" in the Kenyan media, her personal blog became a hub for people seeking a fair election and postelection coverage and for family members searching for loved ones, particularly in the Rift Valley. "I was posting updates every hour, every two hours, and it got to the point that if I didn't blog, people were like, hey, what's going on? How are you? I'm worried. People were desperate. They couldn't reach their relatives."

Her blog became not only a clearinghouse for crucial information, but as only one woman writing and editing content, it also became a "choke point"—a bottleneck to the flow of information. She wrote on her blog that there must be a better way to crowdsource citizen journalism and crisis reporting. "My firstborn was only ten months old," said Okolloh. "It was indeed a tough decision as I went to stay in Kenya until the crisis was resolved, in order to help get information about what was going on out there. I insisted that my husband take our child and return to South Africa, but he wouldn't hear of it." In the end, Okolloh decided it was best to return to Johannesburg, but what she had experienced remained at the forefront of her mind. It was on the flight back home that the idea of Ushahidi came to her. The idea was for people to submit reports directly to a site where the reports could be mapped using whatever tools worked for them—web or mobile.

A group of programmers joined forces with her and helped her build and launch Ushahidi, which means "testimony" in Swahili. Since then, the platform has been used to gather, map, and disseminate information in situations ranging from the conflict in Syria and the Congo to the 2010 "Snowmageddon" in New York City and the devastating 2011 earthquake and tsunami in Japan.

In the three years that Okolloh spent fundraising, building, and scaling Ushahidi, she worked out of her bedroom—hardly an easy task while raising children who would sometimes ask to come in and make a cameo appearance on her Skype calls.

"The practical challenges included the loss of income. I had to quit my job to make this thing happen," she said. "Then there was all the guilt associated with juggling motherhood and the demands of a startup. But I was fortunate, first of all, to have had a very supportive husband, partner, father of my [now] three kids. And so in that sense Sheryl Sandberg is right—your partner really helps to frame a lot of these things."

After Ushahidi, Okolloh went on to become Google's policy manager for Africa, concentrating on issues of access, since the 2013 data provided by the International Telecommunications

Union in Geneva showed that 2.7 billion people (nearly 40 percent of the world's population) were online, but only 16 percent of the African continent were Internet users, compared to 32 percent of the Asian continent and subcontinent, 61 percent of the Americas, and 75 percent of Europe. Her focus was now to foster relationships between Google and African governments in countries where Google had offices: Senegal, Nigeria, Kenya, Uganda, Ghana, and South Africa and work to create a favorable regulatory environment for the burgeoning technology space in the continent.

"From Google's perspective, the more Africans online, the better. Google wants more people using their products," she continued, "so they are willing to invest in infrastructure building and local content in order to get more people online."

In the meantime, Okolloh was becoming an expert on what life/work balance meant to her in the context of being ambitious, entrepreneurial, and socially conscious. Certainly, working for Google was intense, but she was also able to manage her own schedule by frequently working from home.

Asked about where her interest in technology came from, Okolloh pointed to her time at Harvard Law School and the Berkman Center specifically. "At the time, Berkman was attracting a lot of stars," she said. It was a virtual Who's Who of the Internet, blogging, tech conversation, and community spheres—among them, Rebecca MacKinnon, who had joined the center as a research fellow and founded Global Voices Online in collaboration with Ethan Zuckerman; Andrew McLaughlin, also a fellow at Berkman, who would soon leave his job of five years as director of global public policy at Google to become part of President Obama's transition team in the Technology, Innovation, and Government Reform cluster (he would go on to become the administration's deputy chief technology officer of the United States); and David Weinberg, an American technologist, also a fellow at Berkman, who was best known as the coauthor of The Cluetrain Manifesto, the 2000 classic primer on Internet marketing.

In the spring of 2013, she joined the Omidyar Network,

a nonprofit run by eBay founder Pierre Omidyar. Her role as director of investments focused on Internet policy, government transparency, and citizen engagement in African nations, including open data movements. "We as Africans are well-positioned to help investments go to the right areas, and we need to make sure that, as the continent begins to facilitate a global dialogue regarding its investment potential, we're not cut out of the conversation," she emphasized. Women like Ory Okolloh were showing that the female presence in technology was not just reshaping how the world operated, but also growing the connections between entrepreneurship, problem-solving, and global awareness.

Life Lessons from a Mexican Village

LETICIA JÁUREGUI CASANUEVA

Leticia Jáuregui Casanueva is the founder of Crea Comunidades de Emprendedores Sociales, a company that trains and advises low-income female microentrepreneurs in marginalized communities to strengthen and grow their businesses.

Around the world, women are disproportionately affected by poverty and inequality; they stand at the crossroads of economic growth and human development. In the case of Mexico, many women are pushing their cultural boundaries and setting up micro and small businesses to help lift their families out of poverty and ensure a better future for their children and their hometowns. While doing research in poor rural areas of Mexico, I met Rita de Luna Calderon, who challenged her place in society and became a successful entrepreneur and a role model for many other women in Mexico.

Rita had three girls and became a widow. She then realized she had to provide a living for her girls, but more than that, she wanted to make sure they'd have the opportunity to get educated and have a better future. She started off by borrowing her mother's tortilla mill and making pinole, an Aztec energy drink. Very quickly the demand for it increased, and she decided to develop new products and seek out new clients. She developed a reputation in her area and got an invitation to present her products in a trade fair in Mexico City. This was the motivation she needed to grow the business. She also realized women could be entrepreneurs, and she could both care for her daughters and have a business that could pay for their household expenses. On her own, she was able to improve the recipes for her products and increase her production volume. However, she lacked business tools and practices that could help her grow at a faster pace, innovate, and integrate technology and investments into her company.

Women like Rita inspired me to do the work I do: help women in marginalized areas become successful entrepreneurs, leaders, and decision-makers. I grew up with great privilege, and I wanted to share the resources and opportunities I've had access to with other women. It levels the playing field for all of us to actively participate in the economy. I've leveraged my skills and academic background to develop a practical and personalized training methodology into basic tools that these women need to run their day-to-day business operations more effectively. I've used my contacts and social networks to create a network of mentors, business advisors, and supporters who help me envision high-impact strategies and long-term goals for these women. Finally, my resources have opened new markets for women's products.

But how does that translate into concrete results? Rita now has a formal register for her income and expenditures, which has evolved into a digital accounting and inventory tracking system. In the three years we've worked together, she has developed an asset base for her business and has invested in her own machinery. Now she's creating an online presence and e-commerce capabilities for Delicia Jerezana. This has allowed her to improve her packaging, perfect her products, and use technology to integrate new machinery into her production process and access new markets at home and abroad. Her chocolate has been featured in *Saveur* magazine for purchase across the United States.

Rita and her fellow micro and small business owners are the hidden engines of growth in the country's economy. Together we are changing the economic landscape of marginalized Mexican communities. Women-owned businesses reap large social dividends through investments in health and education, for example, yet women are less likely to own businesses, and their businesses tend to be smaller and slower growing than men's. In Mexico, 36 percent of microenterprises, close to two million companies, are owned by women. Unfortunately, in a vast majority of states, close to 90 percent of microenterprises generate annual revenues below $10,000 and fail the first year. My goal was to revert that failure rate by fostering a thriving ecosystem that would allow these female entrepreneurs to grow and succeed.

Today, after five years, I can proudly say that I have turned that failure rate around.

But what is the landscape like for these businesses? Let's start with the cultural barriers these women face. First, there is still a strong macho culture in Mexico, especially in rural towns, which prevents girls from completing their education. This leads to gaps in labor market opportunities and wages. In addition, the main barrier to growth of microenterprises in marginalized areas is derived from a lack of business and entrepreneurial culture or networks, leaving women without role models or access to information that is key. This in turn prevents women from accessing training in business administration and business development services, leaving women without the skills and management tools or information on how to become competitive; and technology and ICT tools, leaving women with limited access to information, new markets, and more efficient and innovative ways of conducting business.

There is a lot to do, and there are new ways in which we can continue to use technology as a facilitator to enable these female entrepreneurs to thrive. And it is relevant for women across all of Latin America. I am excited about the opportunities and the work I can do to impact the lives of millions of women around the region.

Giving Back

When we asked our contributors for the names of women they especially admired who applied technology to problem-solving, they cited (among others) Mari Kuraishi, cofounder and president of GlobalGiving.org; Jessica Jackley, cofounder of Kiva.org, the microfinance and antipoverty organization; and format-breaking pioneers like Tiffany Shlain, who specialized in "cloud filmmaking"—using crowdsourced video to create a new type of collaborative film to help nonprofits. Shlain cofounded the highly influential Webby Awards and made the award-winning feature documentary, *Connected*, which tells the story of how humans shape and are shaped by technology. Through her filmmaking and the footprint of the Webbys, her impact on connecting wider audience participants to an evolving digital world cannot be minimized.

The mother of two children, Shlain said, "The Internet has allowed me such freedom to make a big impact on the world while also being a very present mother. I think the web in many ways is very feminine. At its best, it's collaborative and inspires empathy."

She recently participated in a project that brought global thinking to new heights—literally. UnGrounded was a summer 2013 adventure sponsored by British Airways and the United Nations—an innovation lab in the sky. One hundred participants, including Shlain, flew from Silicon Valley to London, using their hours in the air to brainstorm. Her task was to expand the scope of STEM and ways to teach it.

"I think that learning computer code should be a required language. Every child should learn how to do it alongside learning English. It's the new official second language of the twenty-first century," she said. "But in addition to coding, I think there's a set of twenty-first century skills that should be celebrated and taught in the school system. Logic, how to fail, how to iterate... We also strongly support adding the letter "A" [for Arts] to STEM [to make it "STEAM"—which others, including musician Yo Yo Ma, endorse] because infusing science, math, and engineering with art will bring the necessary emotional engagement that's missing when we teach math and science in the classroom."

As director of public policy for Girls, Inc., Andrea Wolf ran a STEM education advocacy program called Operation Smart. She said, "Oftentimes women want to know *how* they're helping people. How is it that computer science, or electrical engineering, or chemical engineering *helps* anyone?"

Loretta McCarthy said she also noticed that female entrepreneurs tended to approach entrepreneurship with a problem-solving focus rather than a passion to come up with a "cool idea." For example, Playrific is a media channel/curation tool for children created by Beth Marcus, a successful serial entrepreneur who wanted better game and video content for her daughter. She raised $1.7 million in a 2012 investment round led by Golden Seeds.

"The thinking of where and how to innovate is often informed by the life experience of women entrepreneurs. They might propose a technology solution that would greatly improve the efficiency of how something gets done," said McCarthy, "or it could be something that just broadly makes the world a better place, such as health care payment processing, or the whole genome area. I can't explain the psychology of it, but it is less likely, I think, to see [women] entrepreneurs create a technology with an undefined purposed that they hope will just catch on."

Mary Grove, director of Google Entrepreneurs, said, "Entrepreneurship is thriving in all corners of the globe. I've been lucky to work with and learn from entrepreneurs in more than 35 countries, and there are some universal qualities among them that we celebrate—passion for a mission, vision behind a big idea, drive to persevere, willingness to sacrifice, fearlessness, curiosity, and having the courage to grasp ideas that seem crazy and game-changing. My parents were immigrants from Thailand who came to America and exemplified the American dream—they ran a business for more than 30 years, which offered me tremendous opportunities while at the same time instilling in me a strong work ethic and the idea that I could create my own reality and do good by doing well."

That said, in speaking with female technologists and entrepreneurs around the world, we realized that not all playing fields were equal—whether we were talking about companies or nations. In 2013, Dell launched the first Global Entrepreneurship and Development Index that tracked women's entrepreneurial potential in countries throughout the world. Among its findings:

1. Countries with the most favorable conditions for high-potential entrepreneurship development in order from highest to lowest were: United States, Australia, Germany, France, Mexico, UK, South Africa, China, Malaysia, Russia, Turkey, Japan, Morocco, Brazil, Egypt, India, and Uganda.

2. Russia had the highest percentage of highly educated female entrepreneurs at 87 percent; Morocco ranked the lowest at 2 percent.

3. Brazil had the highest ratio of female-to-male entrepreneurship startup activity at 94:100; Germany represented the middle at 63:100; and Turkey, the lowest at 29:100.[26]

There was a dizzying amount of data, all of which pointed to the challenges faced and resilience brought to the work of innovation by women.

On our online forum, participants weighed in on the impact of women in the broader innovation sphere. Phaedra Pardue, cloud and content consultant at Sohonet Media

---

[26] "Dell Launches World's first Gender-GEDI Female Entrepreneurship Index," Global Entrepreneurship and Development Institute and The Dell Women's Entrepreneur Network, 2013.

Network, said, "I envision a world where male and female leaders collaborate toward what I've always known as 'the good of all,' where innovation in science, technology, and engineering would be yesterday's science fiction come to life. Welcome to the future, where our children dream of a trip to Mars, and everything is possible, powered by quantum computers that can solve a problem fifty thousand times faster than a traditional computer. One thing that has been revealed to me in the process of participating in this project is that my approach to business and technology is completely feminine. I've always thought of myself as more of a warrior, but I have realized that it's my intuition and collaborative spirit that have given me the most success. Women by nature are receptors. They embrace a problem to solve it. My vision of the future is a world where it's possible to collaborate in order to solve some of humanity's biggest challenges."

Pardue's list of lofty ideas that technology could transform into reality include:

- Quality food supply = No hunger on Earth
- Clean water = Improved health and reduced child mortality
- Open source literacy = Feeding minds that will lead us into the future
- Pursuit of happiness = No slavery and the freedom to choose your own destiny
- End to senseless war, terrorism, and violence = Peace is possible
- Protecting Mother Earth and her precious natural resources = Heaven on Earth

In other words, the women leading innovation today are often passionately interested in the social good (as are many men in the field), and they're willing to stake their own careers on solving social and global problems in an entrepreneurial manner. One of the best examples of this type of work is Acumen, a nonprofit global venture fund that's using entrepreneurial approaches to solve the problems of global poverty. Acumen makes *patient* investments—a term that refers to raising capital, which does not need a quick return, so that businesses can develop services and products for low-income consumers across the world in areas such as global health, clean energy, water and sanitization, and agriculture—in both women- and men-led businesses. When asked for an example of one of its woman-led businesses, Jacqueline Novogratz, Acumen's founder and CEO, spoke glowingly of Kashf—which means *miracle* in Urdu—a microfinance bank for low-income women in Pakistan. Kashf's founder and president, Roshaneh Zafar, worked at the World Bank and started the organization after hearing about the Grameen Bank's work in microfinance.

The origin of Grameen Bank can be traced back to 1976, when Professor Muhammad Yunus, head of the rural economics program at the University of Chittagong in Bangladesh, launched an action research project to examine the possibility of designing a credit delivery system to provide banking services targeted at the rural poor. Muhammad Yunus and the Grameen Bank were awarded the 2006 Nobel Peace Prize—the first Bangladeshi to ever get a Nobel Prize—for their efforts to create economic and social development.

The Grameen Bank Project (*Grameen* means *rural* or *village* in Bangla language) came into operation with the following objectives:

1. To extend banking facilities to poor men and women
2. To eliminate the exploitation of the poor by moneylenders
3. To create opportunities for self-employment for the vast multitude of unemployed people in rural Bangladesh
4. To bring the disadvantaged, mostly the women from the poorest households, within the fold of an organizational format that they can understand and manage by themselves
5. To reverse the age-old vicious circle of 'low income, low savings, and low investment,' into a virtuous

circle of 'low income, injection of credit, investment, more income, more savings, more investment, and more income'

The action research demonstrated its strength in Jobra (a village adjacent to Chittagong University) and some of the neighboring villages during 1976-1979. With the sponsorship of the central bank of the country and support of the nationalized commercial banks, the project was extended to Tangail district (north of Dhaka, the capital city of Bangladesh) in 1979. With the success in Tangail, the project was extended to several other districts in the country. In October 1983, the Grameen Bank Project was transformed into an independent bank by government legislation. Today Grameen Bank is owned by the rural poor whom it serves. Borrowers of the bank own 90 percent of its shares, while the remaining 10 percent is owned by the government. And of the shares owned by borrowers, 97 percent are owned by women.

As the International Labour Office in Geneva puts it, "Microfinance...often targets women, in some cases exclusively. Female clients represent 85 percent of the poorest microfinance clients reached. Therefore, targeting women borrowers makes sense from a public policy standpoint. The business case for female clients is substantial, as they register higher repayment rates. They also contribute larger portions of their income to household consumption than their male counterparts."[27]

Acumen's Novogratz said, "We invested in Kashf when the organization reached eleven thousand clients, to enable it to build another six branches. The bank grew to reach about 300,000 women across Pakistan, particularly the Punjab. Over time, the organization converted its more commercial assets to become one of Pakistan's early commercial microfinance banks. Roshaneh continues to run the nonprofit foundation. I have always felt that she is one of the strongest women leaders I know, not only in Pakistan but around the world."

---

[27] "Small Change, Big Changes: Women and Microfinance," International Labour Office, http://www.ilo.org/wcmsp5/groups/public/@dgreports/@gender/documents/meetingdocument/wcms_091581.pdf.

Novogratz added, "I think one of the most important skills that we develop in this interconnected world is what I would call moral imagination, or the ability to put yourself in another person's shoes. Some might think of it as a soft skill or trait, but it requires deep listening, high order perception, and compassion, which are critical to all leadership in today's world. Women have an advantage—as do all groups that have felt themselves to be 'outsiders.' When rules have not worked for you, you tend to view the dominant world with greater nuance. You tend to 'see' others and how they navigate. Women can also easily find common connection with other women across class, religion, and culture because of so many universal shared experiences.

"A case in point would be a young woman named Emily Núñez. She heard me speak about Acumen at Middlebury College in Vermont and decided that if so many young entrepreneurs could change a corner of the world, so could she. While at school, she started Sword and Plough with her sister. The company uses fabrics from surplus military uniforms, parachutes, and the like and employs disabled veterans to sew beautiful messenger bags, totes, and other terrific items."

Their Kickstarter campaign raised in excess of $300,000.[28] In June 2013, Sword and Plough participated in a "Champions of Change" event at the White House.[29]

On a global scale, Novogratz has been attentive to high-yield, long-range change, the kind that has a deep effect on women's fortunes. "When we look at the most effective high-dividend investments in energy or water, for instance, which provide sustainable services to women in ways they value and can afford, almost immediately you see those women increase their income and their ability to interact," she said. An effective solar light, for instance, can result in cost and also time savings, and both improve women's quality of life.

Currently, a small percentage of Acumen-funded businesses are founded by women, but this will grow as more women are

[28] "Sword & Plough," Kickstarter.
[29] Barbara Miller, "Sword & Plough's Carlisle Founder Gets Award at White House," *The Patriot-News*, June 5, 2013.

educated and trained. We already see a pipeline of amazing female entrepreneurs growing much larger businesses, some of them among the Acumen fellows.

Of importance, as well, is the impact of building companies that provide affordable basic services on the number of jobs created specifically for women. "Most people actually want a job rather than be self-employed," Novogratz said. "For instance, if you look at A to Z Textile Mills in Tanzania," which manufactures bed nets to combat the spread of malaria, "the company has created more than eight thousand jobs. At least 90 percent of them are designed for women." She added, "As entrepreneurs of most Acumen investees grow their workforce, they increasingly look to hire more women, as they see them as more diligent and dependable. One entrepreneur said to me, 'they show up early, they close late. They don't drink as much, and the books are always correct.'"

Novogratz deeply believes in the power and potential of female entrepreneurs as part of this generation seeking better solutions to poverty. This is one reason, among others, that her company has created the Acumen Fellows programs. Currently they operate a global program, with regional programs in India, Pakistan, and east Africa. Women are starting powerful organizations in online education, ethical clothing sourcing, health care, sustainable mining, and sanitation. The companies are imaginative, effective, and they can change the world. And all of them recognize that we will only do so by including all of us, not just half of us.

Anne Hartley, principal consultant at AHC, said, "It seems to me that our ultimate goal and potential as a civilization can only be realized when we have the best-abled minds engaged at the right time in the right place in optimal roles—24/7. Bringing together 100 percent of our best-abled men and women in terms of shared commitment, shared responsibilities, and ownership of outcomes, such that more females are participating professionally in STEM-aligned fields, is how we will close the gender gap in our innovation economy. It means that society and cultures worldwide must free up their women by deeming it acceptable for men to pick up the slack that women have been doing in traditional female roles without penalizing the men professionally and socially."

Maria Thompson of Illinois Tool Works agreed, "We need to celebrate *all* the ways in which women have contributed to furthering society, creativity, and innovation. They do not have to win a Nobel Prize to be a role model for younger girls and women. Every successful woman has skills to teach the younger generation."

Homeward Bound—
Celebrating Future Makers

LAKSHMI PRATURY

Lakshmi Pratury is the host and curator of the INK conference (www.INKtalks.com). She brings with her a varied and rich experience that spans across for-profit enterprises (Intel), venture capital firms (Global Catalyst Partners), and nonprofit organizations (American India Foundation). Featured in the list of "100 Most Powerful Women" by Forbes Asia in 2010, Lakshmi has traversed an incredible distance professionally. Lakshmi was a topper in the University (gold medal), graduating with a bachelor's degree in mathematics from Nizam College in Hyderabad, India. She attended IIT in Mumbai, has an MBA from the Bajaj Institute in India, and a second MBA from Portland State University in the United States, with a minor in theater arts.

My father told my two older sisters and me that none of his daughters could get married unless they had their master's degree. He gave me the freedom to learn whatever I wanted, wherever I wanted. From Hyderabad to Mumbai to Portland to Silicon Valley—he cheered me on and never demanded anything, except a weekly three-minute phone call.

As I climbed the professional ladder in the United States, my connection with India was reduced to the two weeks I would spend there on vacation every year, mostly shopping and visiting family. As I enjoyed the fast-paced life of an executive at Intel

Corporation, my father visited me in the United States. He was very impressed by my job, with my hallway introductions to our then-CEO Andy Grove and chairman Gordon Moore, with my four-bedroom condo that I bought as a single woman, and with all my friends from diverse backgrounds. But what started as a vacation ended in a major tragedy when my father went into a coma from a respiratory failure. I thought of all the things I wish I had said to him, and I was shattered, watching him lay still in ICU.

In a miraculous recovery, my father came out of the coma after nearly six weeks—it was as though he died and came back alive. We had the most amazing time through his recovery for the next six months. We had discussions on diverse topics ranging from my disastrous first dates to the dilemmas I faced at work. He helped me make up my mind to marry my best friend. After five weeks of preparation, we were married and my father gave me away. As my father prepared to go back to India, he said that he was really happy with my life in the United States and that he had no intention of asking me to return to India. But he asked me, "What are you doing to bring the richest democracy, the United States, and the largest democracy, India, together?" I did not have an answer, but the question haunted me.

On December 15, 1997, I got that dreaded phone call from India saying that my father was ill. By the time I reached home to Hyderabad, he was gone. As I sat next to his funeral pyre, all my professional achievements seemed irrelevant. I felt terrible that I was not with him when he needed me most. Here was a person who went to jail to fight for India's freedom, who lost his wife in his forties and raised his three daughters as a single parent, who dedicated his life to being a pediatrician, who gave me everything I ever needed even before asking—and what was I doing to repay him for all that he has done for me? I wanted to do something, but wasn't sure what.

In 1999, I quit Intel and started my journey to reconnect with India—first as a venture capitalist and then as a social entrepreneur, I traveled the length and breadth of India. In 2001, I cofounded a program called "Digital Equalizer" that brought Internet connections and computers to under-privileged schools across India. I was blown away by the shift in confidence and ambition demonstrated by students when they had access to information. I was also touched by the stories of the indomitable human spirit. I was dissatisfied with the stories that were told about India. The global stories were either about poverty or the richest people, about outsourcing or economic indicators. They were not capturing the spirit of the youth, the local innovations, and the journeys behind the success. I have been attending TED since 1994 and thought that it would be a great platform for me to learn how to tell stories. I cohosted the first ever TEDIndia in Mysore and witnessed how great stories bring great impact. First-time speakers on the TEDIndia stage like Devdutt Pattanaik, Pranav Mistry, and Sunitha Krishnan became popular icons online and offline. I felt compelled to move to India to continue the capturing of stories. My husband and I moved to India, along with our five-year-old son.

My journey toward India, which started when I quit Intel in 1999, was completed with my move to India in 2009. It took me ten years and multiple experiments to finally find my calling. I launched the INK conference in 2010, to create a platform to tell the untold stories of ordinary individuals and their extraordinary journeys. What started as an annual conference has evolved into an INK community that is dedicated to celebrating as well as supporting ideas presented on the platform. It has been five years since our move back to India, and even now I have the occasional sleepless night, wondering if it was the right thing to do after an absence of twenty-five years and betting all of our life savings and the resources of trusted investors on this journey. In those fleeting moments of despair, I go to www.inktalks.com and listen to stories of diverse talents that make me glad that we made the move to India.

I want to highlight a few women because when women step off the familiar path, they are "irresponsible;" when they ask for the spotlight, they are "pushy;" and if they speak up too loudly, they are a "nuisance." I have been in institutions and jobs where I was in a miniscule minority—either by gender or by race. It took me a long time to turn things around and treat my minority status as "unique" and move forward with pride. What took me decades to learn comes naturally to these women. They demand their space in no unequivocal terms, completely oblivious to any other alternative. And I love them for it.

Madhumita Halder is an IIT graduate, who worked in the tech industry and then quit to become a teacher for four years. Armed with the knowledge of combining learning with play, she cofounded "MadRat Games," where they designed the world's first Indian language word game—"Aksharit." This has been translated into eleven different languages and adopted by more than 2,500 schools. In the three years since she has been an INK Fellow, MadRat Games has grown and now boasts of hundreds of board games in multiple languages available for all age groups, becoming one of the most prominent companies in the learning space.

Shilo Shiv Suleman is a gifted artist who has a passion for bringing the Indian aesthetic to everything she does— be it designing an iPad app or performance stages, corporate events, or a combination of all kinds. We produced her first app, "Khoya," on iPad and showed the app to Steve Wozniak during his trip to India. He wrote a personal note to her, saying how much he loved it. She sold enough apps to not only break even, but to also contribute back to the INK Fellows program. She launched an artist collective called "Fearless" to condemn violence against women and is now working with other INK Fellows to create an installation for Burning Man 2014.

Sunitha Krishnan runs "Prajwala." After being gang-raped, she decided to dedicate her life to fighting violence against women. She rescues women from trafficking and gives them a home. In her talk, she shared the difficulty of finding a permanent home for these women. We worked with our community and corporate partners and within eighteen months, she had raised enough funds to build a three-acre campus outside Hyderabad. The women take care of the campus with pride and playfulness.

When Sunitha made a full-length feature film on human trafficking, she collaborated with one of the most popular

Bollywood music composers, Shantanu Moitra, who she met at INK. That music went on to win the prestigious national award in 2014.

Each of the victories, connections, and accolades of those who stand on the INK platform give us a renewed faith in the power of stories and the effort that we put in making each voice heard. INK is no longer any one person's journey. A connected community of future makers is shaping INK, and I am thrilled to be part of this family.

When I was growing up, my father used to take me everywhere—from his clinic to his book launches to meetings with politicians. I loved it as a kid and grumbled as a teenager. Looking back, I realize that those meetings, with their diverse sets of people, gave me an education and an extended family that outlasted him. My son is ten years old now and has been a part of my journey since he was born. He travels with me to meetings across continents, silently sucking on his bottle of milk as a baby and keeping himself busy on his Kindle at the back of the room while I have my meetings now. I hope that I can pass on to him the legacy of learning that my father instilled in me, and I hope that it will outlast me.

CHAPTER 5
THE BALANCING ACT

When Sophie Vandebroek was seven, growing up in Belgium, her family took her to her grandmother's house, where there was a television. They woke her in the middle of the night to watch men gambol across the black-and-white screen on the lunar landscape. "I saw Neil Armstrong set foot on the moon, and that was it. I was going to be an astronaut for years." Ten years later, as she was finishing high school, she realized a few things. First, there wasn't really a curriculum at the university. "And secondly," she said, "I thought I wanted a family at some point, and as a girl growing up in a traditional family, my mom stopped working when she got married. And all around me, the mothers are always home, and clearly Mom shouldn't just fly to the moon and leave her kids and husband home alone. And so I became an engineer and focused in microelectronics, and then life went on from there."

At engineering school in Belgium, then-Sophie Verdonckt had started dating Bart Vandebroek, the man who would become her husband. They married before leaving for the United States. They both attended Cornell University—he for an MBA, she for a PhD in microelectronics, working on chip and processor design.

Then, suddenly, Bart had a fatal asthma attack while the family was camping. Vandebroek was left with three young children, no family in the United States, few friends, and not much money. Bart, who was just 34, had no life insurance, and the family had to get by on one year's salary from his company.[30]

---

[30] "Making It Work By Not Doing It All," *Businessweek*, March 19, 2006.

Faced with this kind of scenario, no one would have blamed her for slowing her career, returning to Belgium, or both. Instead she rose to become the current chief technology officer at Xerox, overseeing hundreds of researchers. She works on innovation around the globe, not only in printing but also in health care, transportation, customer care, education, finance, and more. When her husband died, Vandebroek said, "I was a second line manager at the time, a research lab manager it's called. So I was already leading a team of about thirty people. The first thing my boss said, trying to be respectful and nice: 'Sophie, please, just work for me. Somebody else can manage your team. You don't need to worry about that.' And I said, 'But, Joe—my work, that's where I can forget about all the mess at home. I love my work. Don't take that away from me; it's kind of like my anchor, it's my stability.'" She realized most of her friends from home had stopped working and become stay-at-home mothers. They were living such different lives than she was then as a single parent and sole breadwinner. Vandebroek downsized her household expenses and took stock of what else she needed to do to cope.

From the devastating experience, Sophie relearned how to invest deeply in a career that was important and ramped up her self-care, including taking time to exercise. She also delegated tasks that others could do. "For twelve years, I raised my kids alone, and my priorities were time with my kids and then doing a good job at work. But everything else—cleaning, grocery shopping—I delegated." People think she can afford to do that because she now has a high-paying top tech job. But Vandebroek said she delegated from her first job, hiring students to pick her children up from school, do laundry, do grocery shopping, and get dinner done. In some ways, the work that Vandbroek hired someone to do indicates just how much work-outside-of-work employed mothers and fathers have to take on. She also urges, in general, resisting the cultural drive to buy a house bigger than you need or expensive items that aren't really going to make you happy. "Really simplify," she said. "And if you can simplify, that will create more money to also delegate."

Vandebroek has been remarried for five years. For her, scientific pursuits and other life challenges are part of a healthy, happy approach to life. "Fun is maybe the wrong word, but it's important that you are happy and that you feel good. And that's a combination of both work and life. That unless you're happy at home, you won't be happy at work, and unless you're happy at work, you won't be happy at home. At home, you have to make sure that you have a best friend, often your partner or your spouse, because otherwise life gets way too lonely."

The Misadventures of Motherhood and Management

S. Mitra Kalita

S. Mitra Kalita is the ideas editor at Quartz, the global economy startup of Atlantic Media, and the author of numerous books. She worked previously at the Wall Street Journal *from 2008 to 2012, first as deputy global economics editor, then as senior deputy editor, and finally as senior special writer. She also launched Mint, the second largest business paper in New Delhi, and became its national editor and columnist for two years.*

In one of my first newsroom jobs, I had this amazing editor. She talked to me every morning and would take kernels of observation and help me shape them into real stories. She'd respond to my weekend or even middle-of-the-night e-mail pitches with great enthusiasm. She sheltered me from other managers asking for busy work and encouraged me to keep thinking big.

And yet early on in my career, I vowed to never be her.

She had three kids but *worked all the time.* That was not a life I wanted.

When I moved on to the next paper, I had a similarly fabulous manager, also a woman with two kids. She also worked insane hours, always making time for me in the middle of it all. And again, I said the same—I don't want to be her.

A funny, unexpected thing happened ten years ago: I

got pregnant. And my boyfriend at the time was freelancing and not employed. So quitting and staying home was not an option for me.

These days, as I juggle calls from the nanny, the bus driver, the school nurse, El Salvador's finance minister, and Morgan Stanley's head of emerging markets—and I curse the open office plan that means everyone can hear me—I think back to my vow and smile at how naïve and judgmental I was. Perhaps those yesteryear managers of mine justified their hours because their husbands stayed home, a mother lived with them, their mortgages were huge, or they wanted to set a good example for their kids. I know all these excuses because, by now, I have used them, too. And I, too, *work all the time.*

What I don't think I understood back then is that those women actually *picked* me to join a small, lonely sorority of motherhood and management. All that time I spent judging them was also spent dissecting the juggle: Host the company Christmas party so it can be on your schedule. Work from home in the middle of the week because your kids will miss you less. If you must bring the laptop home, leave the charger behind so there's a limit. Offer every member of your team one day a week she or he can go home early. Schedule conference calls with other mothers at 10 p.m., after everyone's kids are asleep.

I fell into management accidentally, but the fact that it happened to be within a startup was a blessing. When I moved to India in 2006 to launch a business paper, I discovered startups are all in, exhausting, and take a huge toll on family life. But if you are ambitious and want to leave the world a better place (especially for said children), then the decision to join one is pretty easy. They expose merit and work ethic in the purest sense—great for women.

If you work from home (which I try really hard to do the equivalent of two days a week), there isn't as much a question of whether you are actually working or at the grocery store. When I have played more individual contributor roles in larger organizations, it is easier to mask laziness or lack of productivity. And very importantly for women, it's much harder for someone else to take credit for your work when an operation is new, lean, and dependent on breaking old models.

Quartz is my fourth journalism startup (*Mint*, the business paper in Delhi; the Greater New York section of the *Wall Street Journal*; and the New York World, a government accountability project at Columbia University, were the others). Some people might dispute my calling these ventures "startups" since all have been embedded within large institutions and I have no so-called skin in the game. I, too, dream of starting my own company, but have chosen the financial security of my family over those ambitions. (My husband works full-time now, but I remain the breadwinner in our household.)

A certain type of person gravitates toward innovations that attempt to disrupt the status quo. And it's especially hard for women, with the high stakes of leaving a steady paycheck and time with children behind, to embrace risk. When people ask me why I keep doing these new projects, the common theme that has emerged is that women are a necessary part of any industry trying to innovate or reinvent itself. Startups need women. And the ones I have done happen to need me. I hate the term "office mom," but I do think we have this ability to nurture and mentor, give tough love, be blunt in our criticism, and also keep going the immediacy, the need for decisive action and precision. We're good at keeping the trains running *and* figuring out where they're going. So I might not want to be the office mom, but I suspect a lot of women like me look around and are happy to play the role or fill the void that's needed, to do what needs to be done. And startups are all about what needs to be done.

There's a lot of talk in the tech world of needing to "diversify," a code word for the inclusion of more women. Considering we are 50 percent of the population, this euphemism is ridiculous. In my case, race plays a bit of a role, too, because I decided long ago to try to change institutions from the inside out. Since the days of minority scholarship and internship programs in the late 1990s and early 2000s, which helped me enter the newsroom, diversity in the workplace and issues of fairness and representation today actually seem to be getting worse in American institutions, not better. On my worst days, I look around the table, where I might be the only woman, the only person of color, and get pretty disgusted. But then I take heart. At least I'm at the table.

Yet still we remain an afterthought. Companies will set up senior leadership, look around, and *then* realize, "Oh wait, all the jobs at the top are white guys. We need a woman, maybe a minority." Recruitment of diversity in this eleventh hour is too late. It diminishes the role of the last hire and always raises the issue of how "qualified" they are in the first place. That's the worst way to enter an organization.

But beyond workplace culture, there's also an issue I'm surprised doesn't resonate more with managers: the bottom line. I think the fact that tech, for example, skews male means nobody is actually designing products for us (rhinestone-studded iPhone cases don't count as innovation). In my own writing, I've railed against touchscreens as terrible for women who keep long nails. And please, can someone make an iPhone or Samsung that won't break when a child so much as looks at it?

For all their need of women in their ranks, startups are hardly friendly places for mothers. Youthful workplaces have happy hours, late nights, weekends of work. When your children are young, as mine are (ages nine and two), there is no putting them in front of the couch to watch television while you work. They need you all the time. I wonder if my colleagues without children (most of them) have a sense of that. I can be all in, but I can't be always on. I wonder if they look at me and vow never to be me.

Our workplaces don't talk about these divides openly. We don't talk about feeling self-conscious about working from home. We don't mention that yes, we ran out to make it to a soccer game but then logged on at midnight to catch the India team in the morning. We don't talk about how our careers delay family planning or might cause miscarriages. We don't tell colleagues we are pregnant until we are out of the worst of the need for understanding and flexibility.

Indeed, that was the script I once followed. When I was an

editor on a new section of the *Wall Street Journal*, I was six weeks pregnant and nobody knew. I was editing a story about Fashion Week when a nurse called from my doctor's office with bad news: one hormone count was really, really low and it appeared that I had lost the baby. I broke down at work, literally telling my supervisor in a quiet but tearful gush by the coffee machine what had happened. I walked out the door. For three weeks. It turned out I was having an ectopic pregnancy (meaning I conceived in my tube), but until that was diagnosed, I was convinced I had lost the baby from working too hard. My workplace responded perfectly. The executive editor sent flowers and set up a meeting with me; "We'll do whatever we have to do," he said. They asked if I wanted to scale back my role (I did). "You at 50 percent is like most people at 100 percent," one senior editor who took me out to breakfast told me. It was clear that the idea of a woman like me leaving the management track was better than leaving the organization. They did right by me.

But this is where the "not having it all" reality really hit home—I went from manager to reporter. Thankfully I got pregnant again. And had a healthy baby within fourteen months of the miscarriage. I was lucky. After the baby was born, I wanted to stay a reporter, to be there for her. I feared returning to management. And yet I feared not returning.

Once you've had a taste of the power and effectiveness of management and know you are good at making things happen, it becomes hard to stay sidelined. But those bigger roles are hard to do with children because they demand face time and real leadership and being "all in." When I directly supervised twenty-two people (the most I have ever managed), I took home all their problems with me and fretted over their stories, their futures, their careers, their breakups. I tried to do what those managers who helped me along the way did. Unlike my husband, I don't really shut off when I come home. It's a good and bad thing.

So last summer when I got a call to join Quartz, the global economy site of the *Atlantic, and* be in senior management *and* work from home a few days a week *and* still write books *and* still teach, I took it. But somehow I think women feel we should be grateful to be accommodated. I concede I am self-conscious of having a "deal." I think a white guy in my position would think the organization would be grateful to land *him*.

When Quartz launched, I was still pumping breast milk for my daughter. We had a retreat in our president's apartment. I pumped in his master bedroom. We went out for a Chinese banquet dinner. I pumped in the supply closet. We went out for drinks. I pumped in the bathroom. I was determined to be there, though. Those are the sacrifices you make to do it all, have it all.

It's still a really lonely existence. I am constantly looking to infuse our newsroom, and our industry overall, with more female and minority talent. The struggle to do so makes me incredibly grateful to those managers who took such a great interest in setting me up so well, so early on in my career. The least I can do to pay them back is plod on and hope to fill those empty seats at the table.

Career, Community, and Family

While Sophie Vandebroek has dealt with some extraordinary challenges, the fields of STEM and innovation are filled with working mothers—single, married, or partnered. One of the most difficult decisions high-powered women need to make is how to juggle family and other concerns while building a career. Of course, work/life balance is an issue for everyone, not just women with children. Many midcareer workers are dealing with eldercare or simply have other serious pursuits and obligations they have to juggle with their work. Among the issues that emerge when looking at life, work, and family are:

1. Is there discrimination in the field against women with children?
2. What happens to people who leave the workforce and return?
3. And what are some strategies for approaching the mix of roles and responsibilities that being an innovating woman requires?

Different nations provide very different opportunities for women and for parents. Internationally, many developed countries have attempted to address maternity leave in order to remove extended leave as a factor in hiring. Germany has a system called "Eltengeld," which allows a 67 percent replacement rate for previous labor earnings for either father or mother. If both parents participate, they can receive an additional two months, while single parents receive 14 months alone.[31] Sweden offers

---

[31] Jochen Kluve and Marcus Tamm, "Now Daddy's Changing Diapers and

equal parental leave pay to both mothers and fathers, although currently men only make up 24 percent of parental leave.[32]

On our discussion boards, many women encouraged this equal policy as the only way to change views on the gender roles within a family. Anne Hartley said, "Until we get completely comfortable with 'dads' in roles that have been traditional 'mom' roles as the norm, young women who get all the right education and then retreat will continue to feed the gap we are trying to address. When society and cultural norms evolve to where women do not feel that they must 'choose' their place in the family over fully applying their education and themselves for the benefit of humanity or that they are 'bad mothers' to manage their career at the same level of importance as their family."

Gender-based parental leave policies, although helping women spend more time with their children, can prevent a change in mindset as to who is responsible at home. They can also impact company's decisions to hire women who are around childrearing age. "It's time to create better work environments for everyone, rather than singling out women as the ones who need help," said Ellen Pearlman. "Programs identified as helpful to moms or dads end up failing. In order to get buy-in at all levels of a corporation, all workers, from entry-level to executive, must see the benefit of flexibility for everyone." In fact, our Kauffman Foundation research found that 45 percent of female entrepreneurs believe family issues have prevented their female colleagues from founding their own startups.[33]

As we discussed these issues on our online platform, people came forth with stories of inspiration as well as incidents that disgusted them. Rashmi Nigam, a product manager in Los Angeles, recalls working daily from 5:30 a.m. to 5:30 p.m., twelve hours—hardly the work of a slouch. Then her boss ended a conversation by saying, "You basically want a mommy

Mommy's Making Her Career: Evaluating a Generous Parental Leave Regulation Using a Natural Experiment," IZA, October 2009.

[32] "Gender Equality: The Swedish Approach to Fairness," Sweden.se.

[33] Vivek Wadhwa, Lesa Mitchell, Joanne Cohoon. "Women Entrepreneurs in Technology." Ewing Marion Kauffman Foundation.

lifestyle." She said, "My jaw just dropped; I was shocked that someone would actually say something like that in a professional environment. This was the CEO of the company. I have never felt so insulted. I can't imagine that working twelve-hour days would equate to a mommy lifestyle. What exactly does a mommy lifestyle mean?" She decided, "I was done with that company right at that moment. It was the shortest employment I have ever had, and I am so glad I was out of there. In my current employer, although I encourage my team members to bring up their kids, personal lives, I find myself cautious in talking about my life with my higher-ups. I am still so jaded from that experience that I almost don't want anyone to think of me as a mommy."

Many working mothers, including Nigam, have found means of support—either by paying for it, as Sophie Vandebroek did, or by joining with other working mothers. Nigam said, "My husband, my nanny, and I are the three-legged stool that keeps everything together. I often joke, saying that my nanny is my 'wife.' Not sure what I would do without her. The key is to find someone who is just like you are or has the same values as you. I also have an incredible group of mommy friends, without whom I don't know how I would have survived the earlier years of motherhood. I had joined a mommy's group when my oldest was born."

Alice Rathjen said, "I'm a single parent with a ten-year-old boy. The secret to survival for me was to find a core group of parents to help each other out. You get to really bond with more kids than your own and share with others the joy of watching the whole group grow up together." Technology journalist and social media entrepreneur Beth Blecherman found a health club that has drop-in babysitting for her kids. She takes walking meetings (for exercise as well as enlightenment) and works hard to make her children's meetings and sports games. But she also realizes she can't make every one of her children's events, and that's okay. Feben Yohannes said, "The never-ending juggling act that we do as mothers is overwhelming at times, but that process, if channeled properly, is what makes us a creative, resourceful, and dynamic bunch." She is the single parent of a twelve-year-old who she has raised on her own since her child was one. She's also an immigrant without much family in the United States. "I have come to rely on friends and my community for support," she said. "About three years ago, a group of us started a young mother's association, where we meet once a month to ensure that our kids bond and we strengthen our support system. We have a monthly contribution that is set aside for any emergencies. This group and additional other friends have been a huge support in caring for my daughter during my travels."

The Anita Borg Institute for Women and Technology and the Michael R. Clayman Institute for Gender Research at Stanford studied women scientists and engineers at seven large, publicly traded Silicon Valley high-tech firms. Among its findings:

- Many women (and some men) felt there was a career penalty for starting and raising a family
- Some women reported delaying or even foregoing marriage and/or having children to achieve career goals—twice as many as the comparable men
- Midcareer men in the sample were four times as likely as their female counterparts to have a partner who took primary responsibility for the household and children[34]

On our forums, Katie Elizabeth, the CEO of GetGoals, said, "Thankfully, my friends and colleagues (who are all within the entrepreneurial ecosystem) are fully supportive of the (my) entrepreneur's drive to create a successful, high-impact startup and the human desire for companionship and family. Through the long work hours and ups and downs, I have been blessed to be encouraged to give all I need and want to my startup, and also to make time for family, friends, and dating. Balancing creating an innovative, social impact startup with family, friends,

---

[34] "Climbing the Technical Ladder," Anita Borg Institute for Women and Technology and the Michael R. Clayman Institute for Gender Research at Stanford University, 2008.

and dating is not easy. And I will continue to forego marriage for my startup if needed. This said, thanks to many amazing women and some wonderful men who are paving the way, I know it is becoming increasingly possible to create and have both a successful startup and a strong marriage/family."

In some cases, women have found that being their own boss offers much-needed flexibility. Nikki Barua, the CEO of BeyondCurious, a digital design and innovation company, said, "For years, I've struggled to figure out a way to balance my career, home, and hobbies. Something always had to give. It was dealing with the guilt of failing someone—a friend, a relative, a colleague, or myself. No matter how well I managed my time and my priorities, I couldn't get it right. Weekdays were demanding, and weekends felt like time to catch up on my endless list of tasks. Social commitments felt like obligations rather than fun."

Barua continues, "Finally, four years ago, I moved to Los Angeles, quit my job, and started my own company. I still have an intensely demanding work schedule—long hours and lots of travel, much like most entrepreneurs building fast-growing companies. However, for the first time, I've integrated all aspects of my life. Instead of seeking work-life balance, I've unlocked the power of work-life convergence. As my company grew, I hired friends who shared my passion for the business. Now I'm surrounded by my favorite people and don't have to postpone my time with friends. Instead of worrying about dog care, I started taking my dogs to the office every day. My colleagues and I started working out together and planning shared meals that helped all of us to lead healthier lives. I incorporated ways to include my hobbies and personal interests into the workplace. And I created an environment that enabled everyone on the team to converge their personal and work lives. The result is a place where people are happy and thriving. As for me, I finally have a real support system, and I am living guilt-free!"

Elisabeth Hamon, intellectual renewal project manager at SAP, makes it part of her work to support women in general and working mothers. "I'm leading an initiative in the company for women to embrace their careers, and it's been quite successful.

Within eighteen months so far, we have about four thousand women involved from all over the company who live all around the world. Women have less time because very often they have most of the duties at home and with the children." Hamon herself has children and urges women to use all the tools they have at hand—personal networking, tools like LinkedIn, and especially mentoring. "You have to get a mentor. Your manager in an ideal world should discuss with you every few months, 'What are you career goals? Do you need any training?' Things like that." But remember, she said, "Mentors have their own priorities." Hamon tells the women she advises to do the homework so that managers can more easily evaluate requests. "Find out what training you need, why you need it. If you've already done the homework for them, there's a good chance that at least they'll hear it. But if you don't do that homework, they don't have the time to do that either."

Some women, like Holley Zirak, leave their careers for a time and redirect. After receiving an MD in the Czech Republic, she worked at NASA on telemedicine. She met her husband and they had a child together —just as she was ready to start her medical residency. "It was too much," she said. "I was too much in love with this little guy; I couldn't leave him. I started residency six weeks after he was born, and I just couldn't do it. So I left the residency. I was doing family medicine with the goal of doing international medicine afterward, and I had to completely rethink my job and purpose, and what I want, and how can I still really help people in the ways that would really provide me satisfaction and still be a good mum, and still be a good wife and to try to find a balance in all. That was extremely difficult."

"Right now, I do need to focus on my family and giving my children the love that they need," Zirak said. She's currently a stay-at-home mother. In the past, she had an unusual job-sharing arrangement, one that she thinks was particular to her circumstance more than company policy. "When I was at NASA, they were very helpful in allowing me to work from home. I was allowed to just work half-time. That really worked for me, and it really worked for them. They were able to find somebody else to do the other swing hours a week of my job. I delegated certain responsibilities to allow me to work from home, and it just worked really well."

But on a macro level, the question remains: are women still judged harshly for wanting to have both a family and a career? Ellen Pearlman said, "The Pew Research Center just released new findings that show that working mothers are now the primary breadwinners in 40 percent of U.S. households with children; this is up from 11 percent in 1960. But how do Americans feel about this change? According to the Pew study, 79 percent reject the idea that women should return to traditional roles, but only 21 percent said the trend of more mothers of young children working outside the home is a good thing for society. There is, of course, a gender gap in attitudes: about 45 percent of women say children are better off if their mother is home, while 38 percent say children are just as well off if their mother works. Among men, 51 percent say children are better off if their mother is at home, while 29 percent say they are just as well off if she works.[35] Since this trend is not likely to reverse, society clearly needs to address new models for supporting families in the workplace. We are still stuck in the old male-breadwinner model and have not adapted the workplace to such a large number of breadwinner moms."

Nonetheless, innovating working women are finding ways not only to get by, but to thrive as they also face family and life challenges. Sophie Vandebroek believes that Xerox has implemented ways to create a workplace that attracts, retains, and promotes women. It's easier to bring in recent college graduates in a gender-mixed cohort rather than to engineer that diversity later, she said. "In college hiring, which is most of our engineering hiring, well over 40 percent are women. Some years it was even more than 50 percent of our engineering hires were women. As you know, in college, it's about 25 percent [engineering and computer science majors], and in industry, it's about 10-12 percent of engineers who are women. So if you

---

[35] Wendy Wang, Kim Parker, and Paul Taylor. "Breadwinner Moms." Pew Research. May 29, 2013.

can create a culture and environment where people can truly be themselves, they can not only bring their intellect to work, but also their passion and their heart to work. Number one, they'll be much more creative, they'll be much more entrepreneurial. But you'll also be able to attract people from all different colors, from different genders, different ages. We have a very active research group for gay, lesbian, bisexual, and transgender employees. You have to create an environment where people can truly bring their hearts to work, and that will allow you to attract even more diversity and a wide range of people to come work for you."

Vandebroek continues, "Ours was the first company of our size that had a woman-to-woman CEO transition, from Anne Mulcahy to Ursula Burns now. The chief financial officer is a woman. Our corporate controller is a woman. Our chief marketing officer is a woman. Our chief information officer is a woman and again, I'm just going off the top of my head here. I just had lunch with the head of our federal government card business, which is a billion dollar business. She's a woman. So you have many women in leadership roles. Once you've reached a tipping point, again, you can bring your own self. You don't have negative credibility." In the end, she tells innovating women to "follow your heart, not only your intellect, and make sure you really do what you need to do to both be happy at home and happy at work, no matter what big barriers life throws in front of you."

CHAPTER 6
ADVANCING WOMEN

There's no question that while women have advanced (and been held back) within their workplaces, they have also had to respond to the challenges of stereotyping, discrimination, and lack of resources. In nearly all business fields, various forms of intimidation crop up if the rules aren't clear (or are clearly unfair), if the culture doesn't self-examine for bias, and if the companies do not adequately punish bad behavior. The last happened to Quendrith Johnson, the founder and executive producer at Screenmancer.

She said, "In the late 90s, I'd enthusiastically joined a groundbreaking startup that tasked me to do some fantastic projects as well as basic ones. This was an early eCRM [Customer Relations Management] business, and the amazing part was being on a team for a great CEO who let us all have a say in the design of a custom interface. This should have been a happy story. But as my expertise and experience began to result in promotion and respect, a head sales guy just decided to bury me. In a meeting with his lackey, while he wrote on a whiteboard, he turned to me and asked out of the blue, 'Do you ever sleep with anyone besides your husband?' Hello, what? He even repeated it for me, when asked. Brazen and undaunted after my complaint to the CEO, the guy literally bumped my chair every day, several times, and harassed me to no end for reporting this. Then came war. They told me I could quit. They stripped me of my stock options, or tried to—until the most amazing woman backed me 100 percent. Her name is Lois Cox [a pioneering female stockbroker]. She was on her way to a pundit gig on The MacNeil-Lehrer News

Hour. She took me to lunch and asked me two questions, which tipped the balance of the scales and my life. The two questions? (1) 'Are you ready to fight?' and (2) 'Are you ready to win?' We won [during arbitration] in a room packed with men."

Consultant Priscilla Oppenheimer said what happened to Johnson after she reported the harassment isn't uncommon. "A lot of women report that they thought they would get help from HR or upper-level management, but they didn't, and in many cases, the exact opposite happened. HR or upper management tried to make it look as if the employee had done something wrong. Organizations are terrified of the bad press and huge expense if an employee successfully sues for a lot of money. In my own case, when I experienced discrimination (an illegally unfair hiring practice), I made a first move at reporting it and was treated just horribly. An upper-level management person tried to come after me for some minor infraction. I'm pretty sure the lawyers told her to do this. They showed their hand. I realized how nasty they would be and left the organization without pursuing action. A lawyer did tell me I had a case, for what it's worth, but he said it would be a huge hassle to win the case. I chose peace over justice."

Women in the fields of technology and innovation have to navigate everything from passive-aggressive bias to full-on raging career takedowns. We need to consider:

- How to identify different types of discrimination and what to do about it
- How workplaces respond
- How other organizations and advocacy groups are changing the culture

Women in the technology industry (and many male-dominated industries) can face everything from the uncomfortable sexual double-entendre (either meant in a genuinely joking way, though still inappropriate, or meant directly to hurt or embarrass a woman), to denial of promotion or hiring, to groping or assault. "Quid-pro-quo" sexual harassment is when an employee is told she (or sometimes he) must offer sexual favors in order to advance. Hostile work environment is another category of harassment that can extend to issues from posting pornography in workplaces to verbal abuse. Of course, one woman may experience more than one form of harassment. Some people will have more or less recourse based on their position within a company's power structure and their personal connections.

Returning to our contributors, Joséphine de Chazournes, senior analyst at Celent, said that early on, she made a choice about how she would operate in a world where quid-pro-quo was an option. "My favorite female mentor told me when I was just out of university and we had just met at a women's network event that I had to decide how I wanted to build my career," she said, "that I would see people climb the ladder in various ways, and that some may go faster than me for non-meritocratic reasons. If I chose the meritocratic path, I had to accept it. I did see one of my bosses who was sleeping with her boss go up [the corporate ladder]...It's easier to accept when you have decided from the start that this was not the way you wanted to do things than if you have never thought about it. It for sure undermined our team," she said. "It also became accepted to sleep with the boss. It set a precedent and was followed by other affairs—all in the open— really 'nocive' for the culture of the company." Although de Chazournes quit her job with the company—and did not benefit from the "non-meritocratic" path—she can respect herself, her career, and her decision; and she maintained her credibility. But it's important not to sugarcoat the issue. Sex sells...and it can sell some careers, at least for a while.

Another form of discrimination happens when women have or are expecting children. In the United States, it's not permissible for an employer to ask if a female candidate is pregnant during an interview, though depending on how soon the baby is expected, it may be easy to tell. And the issue also affects women already in the workforce. Danielle Newman, digital advisor at Closely, Inc., told us, "I was about to get a promotion when I got pregnant, and guess what happened? Yep, never got the promotion... The unwritten rules are the rules." Terri Anderson, director at Anderson Communications, said, "I was advised by an incubator

I was in to not mention that I am a parent when seeking venture capital. I was, and remain, righteously angry about this. How many fathers would be advised the same thing? And my whole product came about *because* I am a parent!"

Quendrith Johnson said, "Once—and this is burned in my brain—a superior told me, 'If your kids were here (closer to work), I would not have hired you.' Comments like this never make the record, a public forum, or get repeated in detail because, while they make laws to protect working mothers, we all secretly know that the unwritten rules are far more stringent and enforceable, even untraceable in any paper trails."

Lynn Tilton was fired from Merrill Lynch and sued for wrongful termination, citing harassment. She said that her supervisor made statements that "her body was voluptuous, that her large breasts were difficult to hide, and that a sexy woman in a work environment made male colleagues uncomfortable." Merrill Lynch denied the charges. The case was dismissed in April 1992 with no judgment for either side. Tilton has gone on to run Patriarch Partners—and remains seen by many as a maverick for daring to file suit.

"I mean, as a young woman on Wall Street, I experienced a lot of sexual discrimination and harassment, and there were all kinds," Tilton said. "Most of it was something that was easy to sort of turn your back to. When your job is threatened, [and there's a question of] whether you will give up your body or not, it's a whole different story. And I got to a point where it was survival being the noblest of my causes. I was so badly beaten by an incident that I didn't think I could move forward in life or take care of my daughter if I didn't fight back. It wasn't someone saying that I had nice legs or my dress was sexy. It was something that was, in my view, sort of life-threatening. Could I go forward? Could I be able to pick myself up?" she muses. "After a couple days, I realized that this was part of my journey, and I needed to be able to fight for what I believe in, regardless of consequence, because it was the right thing to do. It was an important lesson for me—that I would always stand up for principle regardless of consequences, and that would define me."

An African-American Woman's Shock and Dismay in Silicon Valley

TD LOWE

TD Lowe's career began as a risk manager at Fidelity, then a finance manager at Comcast; from there, she worked as a process engineer at AFLAC. Her passion for technology, economics, and solutions served as the inspiration for becoming the founder and CEO of EnovationNation—which provides a new way for startups to protect their intellectual property.

Once upon a time, a little brown girl was born. As a kid, all good stories started with "once upon a time." But my life has been anything other than a fairytale.

Growing up was often hard, as it was for most little girls who love science, math, and science fiction. Like many little kids my age with an inclination toward and fascination with math and science, I wanted to be a Jedi. And not just any Jedi—I wanted to be Princess Leia. As I grew older, though, the images of Princess Leia seemed far from achievable for a brown-skinned girl from Alabama.

Though my hopes of becoming Leia dwindled, it did not hamper my dreams of space. Years later, I read a biography of a very interesting but rather unknown historical figure, Benjamin Banneker. Here I discovered a man who not only dreamed of being an astronomer, but who achieved his dream. So armed with my quest to conquer space (as a Jedi, of course) and my newfound discovery of what was beyond the stars, my destiny was set—or so I thought. I dreamed that I would someday attend Duke University and become an astrophysicist.

My loving mother, having the insight that moms tend to have into the potential of their children, decided when I was in fourth grade to move me to a school that offered better academic opportunities. For the first time in my life, I was in a racially integrated school. Laws had not set segregation—instead, students were zoned to a school based on the community in which they lived. I had to learn swiftly how to strive and survive in an unfamiliar, and at times hostile, environment.

I quickly learned that my voice in my brown skin mattered less than those of my fellow students and that if I wanted to be heard, I had to learn faster, work harder, and be the best at whatever I strived to do. As a result I was selected to participate in the school's honor program, where I was exposed to my first computer programming course. I remember vividly the proud moment when my program was the only one that worked. For the first time, my classmates stopped treating me like an outsider. As a fourth grader, I began to learn that being great in school granted me, as a brown kid, opportunities that were standard for most non-brown kids in my town. Fourth grade opened my mind to a world of possibilities that I had never been aware of.

Year after year of natural science, physical sciences, and rigorous mathematics only increased my love for space beyond Earth. In my high school American History class, I was met with a discussion on innovators that would forever frame my passion for somehow merging the dreams in the colorful George Lucas sci-fi films and my burning love for technology. A student in my class said that she had been taught that it was an African-American slave, not Eli Whitney, who invented the cotton gin. It was an intriguing suggestion, and I began to think, "Could this really be true?" My teacher's response was that, if so, it was the fault of the slave for not claiming credit for his own idea, because he did not have "the common sense to file for a patent."

The blood in my veins began to boil at such an inaccurate portrayal of the historical period. My response to my teacher was that a slave failing to file for a patent had very little to do with common sense. A slave, who was neither considered a human being nor was afforded any rights to the principles of the legal system, would never have had the opportunity to file such legal claims. In that one instant, I understood more about innovation than would ever be taught to me in a classroom. If necessity is indeed the mother of invention, Eli Whitney would not bear the burden of necessity to make the task of picking cotton easier. Rather, it was the nameless African-American slave who had the need.

After a lifetime of having what I thought were fantastic ideas—or at least ideas good enough that others claimed them for themselves—I realized that there had to be a way for people like me to claim our ideas regardless of socioeconomic status. Later, in college, I was introduced to the work of the innovation economist Joseph Schumpeter, who believed that economic growth hinges on innovation and not monetary or fiscal policy.

In early 2010, I began developing my thoughts around how to build the innovation economy Schumpeter spoke of so eloquently and birthed the mission and philosophy for what would become EnovationNation. In December 2011, I was watching Bloomberg West and saw an interview with special guest Vivek Wadhwa. I was so enthralled by his vision of innovation that I was compelled to e-mail a complete stranger to express my sentiments. Unbeknownst to me, I was e-mailing the most caring, generous, and wisest person I have ever met. In less than an hour, he responded to my e-mail. I was in shock, still am in shock, that he reached out to me. We instantly connected and realized that we have a shared vision of what innovation is and how innovation should be promoted and facilitated in our society. He advised me that coming to Silicon Valley would be just the thing needed to carry out the vision I shared with him. On February 29, 2012, I left my life behind in Georgia and moved to Silicon Valley.

The course of my life took me through classes in

international finance, Japanese, Asian studies, and economics, only to return me to the thing that I have most loved: technology. What I learned was that the warm feeling sparked in my heart had a little less to do with the stars and space itself (although I must admit I seem to still have something of an infatuation). The true spark was one hologram and one famous line from that very special movie that made George Lucas my hero. I knew then I wanted to be a part of a future where technology that existed in Star Wars would be a part of my everyday life, and coming to Silicon Valley would make that dream possible.

I arrived in the Valley bright-eyed, a somewhat naïve optimist believing that for the first time in my life I had come to place where neither my gender nor my skin color would matter. All that mattered would be the gray matter between my ears. Growing up in Alabama and being taunted my entire life for simply being who I am, a brown-skinned girl who loves Star Wars, football, science, and guitars, I learned to survive in very hostile environments. Later in life, on the same campus of the University of Alabama where a governor once declared that racial segregation would live forever, I learned to walk with my head held high. Even when I have heard the N-word hurled at me from unidentifiable faces in a crowd, never once did any of it cause my feet to falter. Little did I know that my dream of Silicon Valley, a place showcased as a true meritocracy where discrimination does not exist, would swiftly become a sight as familiar as my experiences in Alabama.

Where I grew up, being black was the worst possible thing you could be. In the south, being a woman was secondary to race. My entire life prior to arriving in Silicon Valley had been consumed with overcoming discrimination. I studied economics in college, a field of study that women don't tend to gravitate toward, so I was often the only woman in male-dominated classrooms. But attending the University of Alabama meant that being brown-skinned trumped my gender.

Three days after arriving in the Valley, my hopes of living in a new free world were quickly deflated. I attended an event sponsored by a very large search giant. I was new to the area, but I began to hear buzz in the room that a very high-profile investor and incubator founder was in the room. Everyone was making the rounds to meet him, so I thought that this was my first and best chance to go over and introduce myself. I waited while others before me talked and engaged with him. Then I walked up and introduced myself. When I reached out to shake his hand, I got a lukewarm response, and then, before I could even begin to share why I was there and what my startup was all about, he told me that the best thing I could do was to forget startups and get a job. He insisted that I would never be able to make the right connections to be successful in the Valley. I walked away stunned. This place had been painted as a utopia for intelligent people with good ideas, so I came to Silicon Valley, only to discover that there was little difference from the South I left behind.

I later learned that this gentleman was publicly accepted as an advocate of women in technology, but my personal experience with him proved otherwise. It was an awakening to what I would face repeatedly in the Valley. I once watched an associate of a VC firm engage every man in the room, but when I attempted to speak with him, all he did was ask me repeatedly, "Are you sure you are a developer?" As if being a woman automatically excludes me from having the technical skills to develop. I have experienced this same discrimination at tech conferences, male-led Meetups, and tech networking events. Even a representative from a very prominent company running a booth at a large tech conference repeatedly asked me if I was sure I understood what SDK stood for. He spoke to me as if I were a kindergartner. One of my team members, a man, was so offended that he later said to me that he was angry that I didn't tell someone that this happened.

It took me about forty-eight hours to recover from the initial incident, but subsequent incidents have become much less scarring. Although I have been called the N-word by my college classmates, in department stores, and heard it screamed by people driving by, this first incident of being treated poorly because I'm a woman was far more devastating. I was raised with the expectation that I would experience hate in the South, but never did I expect to come to a place as highly educated as Silicon Valley and experience discrimination. Here I am the W-word: woman.

I've spent my whole life compensating for my brown skin by working harder, studying more, and going above and beyond to excel at everything. But upon my arrival in Silicon Valley, I was ill-equipped to fight the hurdle here of being the W-word. My grandparents taught us as kids that it doesn't matter how far you fall, but rather how quickly you get up. At the end of the forty-eight hours, I knew I had to get up. I rose with greater determination than ever to prove this person wrong. Fairly or not, I've had to develop immunity and am daily developing skills to combat being the W-word.

In Silicon Valley, I learned fast that it is far worse to be a girl than brown-skinned. I've spent the past year learning to maneuver around the stereotypes that many of my male counterparts have of women in technology. Rather than being angry about it, it makes me more determined than ever to make EnovationNation successful. Skill is universal—opportunity is not. I have dedicated my time and my life to giving voice and opportunity to the unknown people who, out of necessity, innovate and invent, to forge a true meritocracy where a person's skin or gender is invisible, and only the quality of their ideas matter. The barrier has always been that only the male elite or the financially wealthy could afford to participate in, or claim credit for, innovation. So my challenge is to create a way in which all sectors of society, both big and small, can participate in innovation and experience the merits of adding innovation to society, all while adding value and continued growth to our business sector.

The Female Tax

For many of the women on our forums, questions of appearance were a career issue separate and apart from harassment. Brooks Bell, founder of a self-named enterprise-level testing and optimization firm, said she calls it the "female tax" because compared with men's grooming responsibilities, women need to do everything men do career-wise AND:

1. Wear a bra
2. Put on makeup
3. Wear fitter [i.e., more tightly fitting or tailored] clothing
4. Often wear heels
5. Do our hair
6. Moisturize
7. Stay in shape
8. Keep our wardrobe in style

She added, "All women recognize the importance of appearance, but it's still taboo to recognize how important it is in the workplace and for our careers. When I've advised younger women that how they look matters, I usually get an uncomfortable and awkward reaction because it seems a little sexist to suggest that their value is in their looks."

Catherine Rose, senior product manager for LightAide at Philips, admits: "As far as my inner self—I really do hate dressing up and fitting into the system at the office. I have a PhD in Engineering, then an MBA, which means that I would rather people value me based on my contributions instead of my outward appearance. I do recognize that I should put on makeup and get dressed up, but I would rather spend my time moving projects forward."

Jex Musa, who runs a connection and headhunting firm ByJex, said, "Physical appearance makes a huge impression on the people you work with. It's your first impression, what you're saying to the world about how successful you are and how successful you want to be. I believe my personal style has helped me.

"I don't doll myself up with a ton of makeup every day or wear stilettos. I dress with precision and style, though. I know that if I show up to meetings wearing flip-flops and a T-shirt, I will be taken less seriously. Unfortunately, many men I know DO show up in flip-flops, and people take them just as seriously.

"Women are judged a bit more harshly (even in the startup world), and there is still the expectation that they look 'pretty' or 'professional' each day. Because there are so few women in my industry, each one is noticed and critiqued even more strongly."

Letting Women Do Their Jobs

KIM POLESE

Kim Polese is Chairman of ClearStreet, a financial wellness company that helps people save money and achieve longterm financial health. Ms. Polese has a deep track record of technology innovation. She began her career at IntelliCorp, helping Fortune 100 companies use AI expert systems, and later moved into product management at Sun Microsystems where she led the launch of Java in 1995. She then co-founded Internet software pioneer Marimba, serving as President, CEO and Chairman and leading the company through IPO and a successful acquisition by BMC. Ms. Polese advises numerous technology startups and serves on several boards, including the Silicon Valley Leadership Group, TechNet, the Public Policy Institute of California, the University of California President's Board on Science and Innovation, and the Long Now Foundation.

My path to computing started early. I grew up a "girl geek" in Berkeley, California. Encouraged by my immigrant parents, I developed a love for technology from an early age, entering science fairs, fascinated by space exploration, and imagining the world of the future. Nearby was a place called the Lawrence Hall of Science, a science museum overlooking the San Francisco Bay, where I spent many afternoons growing up. Among the many exhibits was a mainframe computer that ran a program called Eliza. Eliza was a virtual psychotherapist. I'd sit down at the computer, and the computer would type a message: "How are you feeling today?" I'd reply, typing my answer, and Eliza would respond, asking me why I felt that way, and before long, we were having a conversation. At the time, I didn't know that Eliza was one of the first Artificial Intelligence (AI) programs that demonstrated natural language processing. As a young girl, I spent hours "talking" with Eliza, often testing "her" limits by forcing Eliza into a semantic dead end. I was fascinated by what was behind the screen. How did the software work? And what was software anyway? Because of Eliza, my first interaction with computers was not only a positive one, but it also set me on a path of exploration and discovery and a lifelong love of computing.

As a freshman at UC Berkeley, I dove into my science classes with gusto and soon became fascinated by the intersection of biological and digital sciences, an area then in its infancy. Not only did I love to code, I found I loved to decode and explain the mysteries of computing, and I began to teach computer programming to kids and adults at the Lawrence Hall of Science. After graduating from Berkeley, I continued my studies in computer science at the University of Washington with an additional year of postbaccalaureate coursework.

By the mid-1980s, when I graduated, the recession had made jobs scarce. I scoured the 'help wanted' ads and found one for an AI software company in Silicon Valley that was hiring technical support people. AI was hot in the 1980s, and the company, IntelliCorp, was one of the fastest growing companies in the industry—the equivalent of working at Google today. I eventually began working onsite with Fortune 100 companies like Ford and McDonnell Douglas, who were using our products to transform their businesses and solve their toughest challenges. It was a phenomenal first job. I was in heaven.

My love for AI led me to join Sun Microsystems three years later. Sun was a fast-growing startup in the Valley that had just launched an AI software business under the direction of Eric Schmidt (now Google's Chairman). I worked on the AI team and then became a product manager for object-oriented software systems. I found that being a product manager was a demanding, but deeply satisfying role that enabled me to work with engineers to design and launch products that helped our customers solve their greatest challenges.

About three years into my time at Sun, I learned about a secret skunkworks project called "Oak," comprised of a team of Sun's most talented engineers. I got a sneak peek at what this team had built and realized that Oak had the potential to revolutionize computing. In early 1993, I signed on as the Oak product manager and moved offsite to the under-the-radar spinoff company that Sun had created to develop this technology. Oak was a software system designed for a networked world that didn't yet exist. It was years ahead of its time—the first web browser had not been developed. Yet our goal was ubiquity—nothing less would do.

As Oak's product manager, my primary job was to figure out a way to convince millions of people to adopt Oak. I felt an enormous sense of responsibility as I realized that the only thing between Oak and ubiquity was me. Over the next two years, we tried various ways to get Oak into the market—from handheld computers (Apple's Newton was state-of-the-art) to set top boxes for early interactive TV trials (the set top boxes were, in reality, $20,000 Silicon Graphics machines). We failed repeatedly because these platforms were too early to be broadly adopted. At one point, I hired a Stanford student to do research on what devices comprised the fastest-growing on-ramp to the "information superhighway." It turned out to be the PC and nascent online services like AOL. So the team created a version of Oak for the PC, but we still didn't have a vehicle to get Oak into the market. By 1995, we were getting discouraged, and we knew our project's days were numbered unless we could figure out a way to get Oak out to the world. Then, at the lowest moment, finally came a breakthrough: the University of Illinois released the world's first web browser, called Mosaic. We downloaded it, and the light bulb went on. We realized that we could introduce interactivity to the web. Up till then, browsers could only display text.

We released our software, which we renamed Java, and along with it the world's first interactive browser, on March 14,

1995 on the Internet. It took off like wildfire, and Java remains the lingua franca of the Internet today, is the foundation of Android, and runs on more than a billion devices.

This is actually a typical story in Silicon Valley—or anywhere that innovation happens. The common theme is persistence. I've learned to never underestimate the power of persistence. And to resist the naysayers. Things generally take longer than you think they should. Your first plan usually doesn't work. Life throws unexpected twists and turns, and factors are outside your control. Our lives end up being defined in large part by how we handle these setbacks.

I like the way Einstein put it best—he said, "It's not that I'm so much smarter than anyone else. It's that I stay with problems longer."

In January 1996, nine months after we released Java, four of us from the Java team left Sun to found our own company, Marimba. Fueled by the vision of Java enabling a new age of network-aware applications, the four of us bootstrapped our startup company, eventually accepting funding from the venture firm Kleiner Perkins. At the request of my cofounders and our new investors, I became CEO, and we built a top team. The first year, we achieved $10 million in sales. By 1999, the year we went public, we were a successful, profitable enterprise software company with nearly $50 million in revenue, competing against the likes of IBM and CA and often beating them in million-dollar deals.

Marimba was one of the first companies to automate software delivery and management over the Internet. At the time, it was a revolutionary concept—delivering and updating software remotely and securely to millions of desktops, servers, and devices. Today people call this "Internet service management" and "cloud computing," but back then it didn't have a defined market segment. So, soon Marimba got categorized into what many began calling "Push." Push was the concept of automatically and proactively delivering software and content, rather than waiting for it to come to you. The excitement about Push reached a high when *Wired* ran a cover that proclaimed, "Kiss Your Browser Goodbye—Push is here."

Because of our notoriety coming out of the Java team, Marimba was a high-profile startup. Among my many duties as CEO, like my male counterparts, I was asked to make keynote speeches at conferences and required to talk with the press. I turned down the majority of the overwhelming number of requests, accepting only those that were necessary. Pretty soon I started to realize that there was a difference in the way Marimba was being covered and the way I was treated as a CEO.

First, in many of the articles there was a focus on me instead of my company. No matter how hard I tried to get the focus on our products, the market, and the future of the Internet, the story often ended up being about me. This created a bizarre situation in which I began to be accused of courting the press to promote myself. The harder I tried to get the focus off myself and onto the company, the more, it seemed, the story was about me.

This was frustrating, particularly because we were building something truly groundbreaking at Marimba. My cofounders were brilliant engineers and had built a remarkable product. We were also one of the few successful startup companies in the "dot-com" era. Our customers were companies like FedEx, Morgan Stanley, and Verizon. But the fact that we were successful got lost in the noise. Soon the press decided that "Push" was dead because a company called PointCast, which was doing something completely different from us—sending sports scores and weather forecasts to screen savers—stumbled. Suddenly, we were lumped in a "failed category" of Push.

At a certain point, I realized it was impossible to change the narrative. But I believed, as I told my team, that as long as we built something of real, lasting value, the facts would eventually come out—Marimba would be known for our groundbreaking products and our customers' success in using them. Our business kept growing. We survived the dot-com bust since we were not a "dot-com," but a successful enterprise software company. Eventually, in 2004, we sold the company for nearly a quarter of a billion dollars to BMC, where its products thrive today, and returned nearly twenty times the venture capital raised.

But somehow that story didn't get told. Instead, another narrative took root—that Marimba was a dot-com highflier that bombed—a failed Push company. I was a PR pro, a publicity-seeker who had been lucky to be in the right place at the right time, and had finally gotten my comeuppance.

The narrative was cemented by pieces like *Fortune*'s 1999 article entitled "The Beauty of Hype." In the fall of 1998, I was approached by a reporter after giving a well-received talk at the Commonwealth Club about the future of the Internet. I politely explained that I was not interested in being interviewed unless the story was going to focus on our company, the technology, and the market—not on me. The reporter assured me this was exactly her intent, and so I agreed. Then, weeks later, just before story before went to press, the reporter called me. "You're not going to like what I submitted," she said. "My editor didn't like the story I filed, and he made me rewrite it."

In a case of hypocrisy so ridiculous that it was almost laughable, this article said virtually nothing about Marimba, our market, our customers, the technology—or anything of substance. Instead it portrayed me as a publicity-hungry femme fatale, with a large photo spread complete with a full-page close-up of my face. Rather than quoting our happy customers or industry sources knowledgeable about our market, the story featured anonymous quotes like, "I don't know what Kim's company does, but I do know she has pretty red hair."

Unfortunately, this was not unusual. There were countless other surreal and bizarre examples. In one case, an online parody "zine" published a fake article about Marimba, complete with a picture of a supermodel with my head Photoshopped onto it. The photo got lots of hits over time, and thanks to the efficiency of page ranking, I still to this day have people compliment me on how brave I was to pose in a bikini!

The examples go on. My strategy continued to be to ignore the silliness, focus on producing results and building great teams and products, and make a real difference for our customers. Eventually, I assumed, the truth would come out. And I figured, in about a decade or so, there would be so many women in the industry, founding companies and leading them, that this silliness would be an anachronism of the past.

After selling Marimba, I became CEO of another startup software company, this one focused on automating the management of open-source software stacks to help companies use open source with more ease. In 2010, I became increasingly interested in applying technology to addressing big social challenges and moved into a role of launching new social impact companies. I became the chairman of a financial technology company called ClearStreet that helps people living paycheck to paycheck achieve lasting financial health. I now advise numerous startup companies in social impact, cloud computing, and data analytics. I mentor many women entrepreneurs and work on bringing technology skills to youth with low socio-economic opportunity.

One day in May 2012, I started getting e-mails from women I didn't know. Many of them said things like, "Don't listen to that guy—you rock," and "You're an inspiration to me." I followed the link and realized that a blogger for *Forbes* online had written a piece criticizing Facebook COO Sheryl Sandberg for supposedly spending excessive amounts of time giving speeches and talking to the press. Entitled "A Cautionary Tale," the writer warned Sheryl that if she didn't focus on the real work of running Facebook, rather than all those self-promoting PR-seeking activities, she could end up like me. A failure, a nobody.

It was another one of those snarky, fact-free pieces, but this time the writer was criticizing another woman leader using those same specious claims. It was too much. I had to finally speak up. A *Forbes* editor reached out to me and asked if I'd write a response. And I did.[36]

The point here is not to complain. In fact, that's the bind women are in when this stuff happens. If you speak up and

---

[36] "Stop Comparing Female Execs and Just Let Sheryl Sandberg do her Job." *Forbes*, May 25, 2012. http://www.forbes.com/sites/carolinehoward/2012/05/25/stop-comparing-female-execs-and-just-let-sheryl-sandberg-do-her-job/

point it out, you end up inviting more criticism—labeled as complaining or whining. But if you don't, than the narrative is repeated unchecked.

Too often it feels like a no-win situation.

But seeing that piece and realizing that not much had changed in the nearly twenty years since founding Marimba made me realize that I, and we, do need to speak out. If we don't, this kind of double standard in judging women leaders becomes institutionalized. And we all lose when that happens. Because we need more women—many more women—to discover that technology is a great career, and found and build and lead companies and develop world-changing innovations.

As it is, we are already graduating far too few computer scientists in America to meet the needs of our economy and society. The U.S. Department of Labor forecasts that there will be 1.2 million computing-related job openings by 2020. At current computing graduation rates we can only fill 39% of these, or 468,000, leaving approximately 700,000 computing jobs unfilled.

Between 2010 and 2020, computing jobs are projected to grow much faster than other STEM jobs and all other professional occupations—a growth rate of 22% in computing, compared to 10% for all other jobs, according to the U.S. Department of Commerce. And incomes for those employed in computing are higher. For example, software engineers earn nearly $100,000 annually according to the Department of Labor and, in general, jobs that require a knowledge of computing come with higher salaries. The impact on lifetime earnings can be substantial.

Economic mobility is increasingly dependent on computational literacy, affecting the ability to thrive in a hyper-competitive, global marketplace. Yet large segments of the U.S. population are significantly underrepresented in computing—specifically, women and people of color, particularly African Americans and Hispanics. And in 2014, with women comprising only 18% of computer science graduating classes, our nation is leaving millions of innovative minds behind.

That's why speaking out about this issue is important. It's not about complaining. It's about shining a light on an issue that is stubbornly persistent and limits economic growth and socioeconomic opportunity, identifying ways to change the status quo, and taking action.

It's a new world. Solving humanity's greatest challenges increasingly requires computational knowledge. The cure for cancer—the ability to develop highly personalized therapies based on our genes—will come from computational biology. The most important innovations in energy, materials, design, manufacturing, virtually every field, increasingly depends on digital technology.

So when women decide that computing and technology is not for them, we all lose. We need as many bright minds inventing the future as possible. We can't afford to let old, outmoded stereotypes affect women's ability to participate in full numbers in the technology industry. The stakes, quite simply, are too high—for everyone.

It's Different for Girls

HEIDI ROIZEN

Heidi Roizen currently serves as the operating partner with leading global venture capital firm Draper Fisher Jurvetson (DFJ). She is also a lecturer at Stanford University and a member of the board of directors of DMGT, ShareThis, Xtime, and Eventful. Roizen was (from 1999 to 2007) a managing director of Mobius Venture Capital and was also elected to the board of directors of the National Venture Capital Association—the largest venture capital trade association in the world—in which capacity she served from 2003 to 2007. From 1996 to 1997, she served as vice president of World Wide Developer Relations for Apple, and from 1983 to 1996, Roizen was cofounder and CEO of T/Maker Company.

Early in T/Maker's life, I was working on a company-defining deal with a major PC manufacturer. We were on track to do about a million in revenue that year; this deal had the potential to bring in another quarter million, plus deliver millions of dollars in the years to come if it went well. It was huge.

The PC manufacturer's senior vice president, who had been instrumental in crafting the deal, suggested he and I sign over dinner in San Francisco to celebrate. When I arrived at the restaurant, I found it a bit awkward to be seated at a table for four yet to be in two seats right next to each other, but it was a French restaurant and that seemed to be the style, so down I sat.

Wine was brought and toasts were made to our great future together. About halfway through the dinner, he told me he had also brought me a present, but it was under the table, and would I please give him my hand so that he could give it to me. I gave him my hand, and he placed it in his unzipped pants.

Yes, this really happened.

I left the restaurant very quickly. The deal fell apart. When I told my brother (T/Maker's cofounder and chief software architect) what happened, he totally supported my decision to bolt.

Years later, we decided to raise venture capital. I was meeting with a Boston-based VC in his office. He had a window behind his head and, unbeknownst to him or the other people in the office, I could see a reflection in that window of what was going on behind my head in the corridor (all-glass offices can be quite revealing in this way). As I pitched him, one of his partners engaged in a pantomime in the corridor, making a circle with the fingers of one hand while poking his other fingers through the circle, then thrusting his hips in a sexual fashion. I found it rather hard to concentrate on my pitch. I did not get a term sheet from that firm.

Luckily, I did get a term sheet from Hummer Winblad—we closed our series A with them, and we continued to grow the business. A few years later, I was pitching our B round at a Sand Hill firm. This time, I was five months pregnant with my first child, so I was pretty sure no one would be doing hip thrusts in the background. The pitch had gone well, and I was meeting with the partner who was going to lead the deal. I was feeling the forward momentum until the partner said the following:

"My partners are concerned that when you have this baby, you are going to lose interest in the company and not be a good CEO. How can you assure us that won't happen?"

I did not get a term sheet from that firm, either. But I did get a term sheet from DFJ, and they and Hummer Winblad went on to get a nice return for believing in me, even in all my pregnant glory. (And this is one of the reasons why I am now a partner at DFJ—I have always found the DFJ crew to be incredibly supportive of women.)

Sadly, I have many stories like the above, and so do my

fellow female entrepreneurs (though I leave it to them to divulge their own).

What's my point?

Just that it *is* different for female entrepreneurs. We face challenges that our male counterparts do not.

So what's a girl to do?

In many situations, my answer is: you have to simply walk away. When I was a CEO, I operated under the principle that if I was not treated properly, it was not worth doing business with the other party. I also believed that if one door was slammed in my face, there was always another door to knock on. I was persistent and lucky—I did find enough other doors that were accepting, and I was able to build a successful business.

It pains and somewhat embarrasses me that I am not recommending calling out bad behavior and shaming the individual or individuals responsible. In a perfect world, people would have to account for their behavior. But as an entrepreneur who spent years in a daily battle for existence, I did not feel like I could afford the hit I'd take in exposing these incidents. (Again, *not* criminal behavior. I suffered a few unwelcome gropes at late-night Comdex parties and the like, but never felt like I was in danger, and I was always able to walk away unharmed.)

I do think things have improved, though of course I'm not an entrepreneur anymore, so perhaps it is situational. I am still (sadly) often the only woman in the room—but my position as a board member in a room full of other board members and senior executives creates an environment where professionalism and civility tend to rule. Plus, let's be honest—I'm now in my mid-fifties, so I have probably gone from the "tempting to grope" category to the "likely to be invisible" category.

I've also developed a pretty thick skin and don't take offense at some things that the me-of-thirty-years-ago might have found offensive. For each of us, there is fine line between things that are colorful but harmless speech and things that are truly offensive. In fact, I've been called out for using the expression "come to Jesus" by a devout Christian and "the pot calling the kettle black" by an African-American entrepreneur—I had no idea those might be offensive to other people. And in my British board meetings, they use the expression "tits up" without a thought that I might find that a bit blush-worthy, and I've learned there's no mal-intent behind their usage, so I just let it go.

That is why I encourage my fellow female trailblazers to look for the intent behind the words. Offensive language is often unintentional, and sometimes you can turn an awkward situation into a bonding experience.

For example, during the dot-com bust, I was a partner at venture firm Mobius and we were dealing with a lot of trauma in our portfolio. We held an offsite with all the deal partners plus our new general counsel Jason Mendelson (now a partner at Foundry and a fantastic venture capitalist and human being). As we reviewed the portfolio deal by deal, many of the deals needed more funding, and at that time no VCs were following anyone else's deals, so it was up to us to decide who would get more dough. Each of us fought hard for every deal we managed. After hearing about a dozen of these pleas, my partner Brad Feld (another mensch and great VC who is also a partner at Foundry) pushed back from the table, stood up, and said, "This is bullshit. Each one of us is just sitting here with his dick in his hand asking for more money without truly justifying it."

Jason looked nervously at me, wondering how I was going to react.

"This is making me very uncomfortable," I said.

"Because I don't even have a dick to hold," I deadpanned.

Without skipping a beat, Brad replied, "Well, if you need a dick to hold, you can borrow mine anytime."

I already knew Brad as a great guy and a huge supporter of women, and I took it for the joke it was intended to be. Everyone laughed. It broke the tension of the meeting and was a bonding moment for us all.

All this leads me to what I consider to be the most important rule about building company culture, but can be applied to the industry at large: Actions are all that matter. How you act—and how you reward or punish the actions of others—will influence how everyone else will act.

So act in a way that's consistent with your values, and try to work with and for people who share those values. Sometimes you'll have control over who you work with, and sometimes you won't. But doing business with high-profile people who don't treat you with respect, no matter how good the press release will look, is only reinforcing the toxic aspects of this industry.

Instead, actively seek out the kind of people you want to work with, allies inside and outside of your organization. It's easier than ever to get to know people from afar on Twitter, LinkedIn, and Facebook, so do your homework. And when you reach out, do it to start a relationship, not to ask for a favor. You need to be the one to invest your time and to connect these new allies when you can, even (especially!) when it's not about you.

The most important thing you have in your life is your time, because while you can sometimes leverage it, you can't make more. And everything takes time. It may feel easier to save your time and ignore a problematic person or attitude in the short term, but in the long term the time spent cultivating successful relationships with people you respect and trust will be worth it.

Sometimes you're going to fail at this because life is messy and failure is unavoidable. Sometimes you never get over the hump, have to work with people you'd prefer not to, don't speak up when you should. But more often or not, you *do* get over the hump. The failures will happen, but the successes will as well—and either way, you'll want to get there with people you're proud to be with.

Boots on the Ground

So what do you do if faced by harassment? Law Guru, which produces briefings on various legal topics, offers a set of basic tips for someone who believes she's experienced harassment or discrimination:

- Tip #1: Collect evidence. How can you ever have a case if you aren't able to prove that you were ever harassed in the first place? There are difficulties with cases in which they could be described as a "he-said, she-said" type scenario: if it's your word against theirs, you don't have a lot of footing to stand on. That's why it's important to gather all the evidence you have available and to document what happened in your life that led you to want to file a sexual harassment lawsuit.
- Tip #2: Find a witness to corroborate your story. It's important that you avoid the aforementioned he-said, she-said scenario by making sure that other people can attest to the harassment you've received. For example, if you are able to identify witnesses that saw and remember you being teased by coworkers on the basis of sex, then those people can add invaluable contributions to your case.
- Tip #3: Talk to a lawyer before making any major career moves. As tempting as it might be to ditch your job and get out of Dodge, you'll want to make sure that you speak with a lawyer about your options before you make any major career or life decisions. You want to know that you have a case—as well as what you

might need to gather in order to build a case.[37]

Of course, not every moment of harassment has a witness, and not every witness will be willing to talk. That's just part of the complexity of reporting an incident or incidents—as well as the question of whether management really has the will to make the situation right.

In the long run, not just direct harassment but also the question of how well women are respected in the workplace makes a huge impression on current and potential employees. Ellen Pearlman states: "There is no question that women have a harder time climbing corporate ladders, but it may also stem from the fact that women don't like what they have to do in order to make that climb. Corporate politics is a turnoff for many women, viewed as a game they don't want to play. I thought that tooting my own horn was unseemly, having learned my lesson well as a child that it's not appropriate to show off. I assumed that good works were their own reward and would be recognized without my having to draw anyone's attention to them. I was wrong about that. In the corporate world, you do have to let the right people know what you and your team have accomplished."

She summarizes some findings from the McKinsey & Company report, "Unlocking the Full Potential of Women at Work." It states: "Among entry and midlevel employees at sixty leading companies, 69 percent of women (and 74 percent of men) had a desire to advance to the next level in their organization. But when asked if anything were possible, would they choose to advance to C-level management, only 18 percent of women said yes, while twice as many men said they would want that advancement. Politics was the most often cited reason for not wanting to go that route."[38] Of course, that's not the only reason we don't find more women at the top of corporations, but until making it into the C-suite looks more

---

[37] "What is Sexual Harassment and Why Do I Need to Know?" Law Guru, July 11, 2011.

[38] Joanna Barsh and Lareina Yee, "Unlocking the Full Potential of Women at Work." McKinsey & Company, 2012.

desirable, it just might not look as inviting to women who are not motivated by money and power alone.

Conferences and industry gatherings can be just as fraught as workplaces. Ellen Ullman, a former programmer turned writer about technology, referenced what happened at the 2013 Python coding language conference PyCon.[39] The conference had made an effort to reach more women, by one account moving the needle on conference attendees from 5 percent to 20 percent over one year.[40] A woman named Adria Richards responded to what appeared to be a sexist or off-color joke by photographing and Tweeting out the images of the men who made it. Subsequently, there was a round of back-and-forth attacks by people supporting Richards and others supporting the two men, and one of the men (who, unlike Richards, wasn't named in current news stories) was fired.

Then came a denial-of-service attack against SendGrid, Richard's employer, and finally SendGrid fired Richards with the statement, "A SendGrid developer evangelist's responsibility is to build and strengthen our developer community across the globe. In light of the events over the last forty-eight-plus hours, it has become obvious that her actions have strongly divided the same community she was supposed to unite. As a result, she can no longer be effective in her role at SendGrid." Some critics then asked why a woman who called out sexism should pay for doing so with her job. (After the incident, though not before, the conference asked participants to report harassment privately.)

Ullman said of Richards and her actions, "I think from a business end, just a professional point of view, you can turn around and say something to somebody and then you have to say in your mind, 'That guy's a jerk,' and just concentrate on what you're doing. I feel for her that she must have been so angry that she was rash. But I have to say what was more significant to me about the picture that she took of these guys is the audience you

[39] Jon Brodkin, "How 'dongle' jokes got two people fired—and led to DDoS attacks."

[40] Nicholas Tollervey, "The Trials, Tribulations and Triumph of PyCon 2013," March 27, 2013.

see behind her. I'm not sure if I can discriminate one woman's face in that crowd. So that's the environment. There were very few women there." She concludes, "Despite this 'Welcome, Women' sign [the conference made an effort to attract more women], what really happens is that there is a 'Boys Only, No Girls' sign on the tree house door."

The industry also needs to create an environment where women are welcomed. In 2010, Noirin Shirley, a writer for Google, wrote a blog post entitled "A Hell of a Time," in which she described being sexually harassed at ApacheCon, a software conference held in Atlanta, her third assault at a conference that year: "I tried to push him off and told him I wasn't interested (I may have been less eloquent, but I don't think I was less clear). He responded by jamming his hand into my underwear and fumbling."[41]

In response, programmer Valeria Aurora founded The Ada Initiative, an organization focused on supporting women working in open source software and data. (According to their figures, only 2 percent of the open source software community are women.[42] and only 10 percent of Wikipedia editors.[43]) The Initiative created a code of conduct for conferences. Remembering what happened to Noirin Shirley, Aurora said, "In 2010, a friend of ours was groped for the third time in one year at an open source software conference. When she complained about it on her blog, it became a worldwide news story—and she was attacked by hundreds of people who told her she deserved to be raped, she was too fat and ugly to be raped, and she was a slut and therefore couldn't be raped."

"My cofounder, Mary Gardiner, and I were horrified and furious. I personally have been groped twice at a conference and harassed too many times to count, but even I was shocked. We

[41] Noirin Shirley, "A Hell of a Time," http://blog.nerdchic.net/archives/418/, November 5, 2010.

[42] "Women, Minorities, and Persons with Disabilities in Science and Engineering," National Science Foundation, NSF04-317, Arlington, 2004.

[43] Ayush Khanna, "Nine out of Ten Wikipedians Continue to be Men: Editor Survey," Wikimedia Foundation, April 27, 2012.

talked about the problem and decided that we needed to educate conference attendees about what behavior was acceptable, give conference organizers guidelines on how to respond to harassment, and give potential attendees an idea of how likely they were to be harassed at a particular conference and what the organizers' response was likely to be. We made it easy by writing not only an example code of conduct, but also a lot of supporting resources on how to take harassment reports, how to respond, how to tell attendees about the code of conduct, lists of conferences with codes of conduct, etc. These are all available for free and editable on the Geek Feminism Wiki."

Her advice to conference organizers is direct:

1. You need to tell the attendees about it: put it on your website, include it in e-mails, print it in the program booklet, and announce it in the opening session each day. I know several conferences that have a secret code of conduct; this doesn't help much if your attendees don't know what standards of behavior are acceptable.

2. You also need to train the conference staff on why stopping harassment is important, what harassment is, how to take reports, how to respond, and when and how to make public statements about an incident. These have to be worked out in advance; often the time frame for responding to an incident before a public outcry is only hours long, and many people are in shock and not thinking clearly when an incident happens.

3. Most importantly, the policy must be enforced. This is very difficult for most people because many people avoid conflict, but without an organizer willing to enforce the policy, the victims of harassment don't have a choice about getting into conflict.

4. Conferences should also avoid "high-risk activities": activities that encourage people to view women as targets of harassment. Unfortunately, many cultures

view drunk people as not responsible for their actions, despite research showing that drunk people behave very differently depending on cultural expectations. In cultures where being drunk is an excuse to be violent or sexually harass people, drunk people do those things more often. In societies where that isn't acceptable, drunk people often giggle a lot and then fall asleep. Limiting the number of free drinks at parties or just establishing a sense that being drunk is embarrassing and unprofessional make a big difference in rates of harassment.

Aurora also speaks to what is sometimes (and controversially) called the "booth bunny" phenomenon at tech conferences. "If female booth staff on the convention floor are overwhelmingly hired for their sexual attractiveness, while male staff are hired for their knowledge, it sets up an expectation in attendees that women attending are not colleagues but objects for the enjoyment of (presumed straight male) attendees."

The end result of unchecked harassment is a loss for women in the field and a loss for the field itself. "Harassment and assault absolutely discourage women from attending conferences," said Aurora. "I know dozens of women who stopped attending one particular computer security conference because of the near constant harassment. Not every woman will give up. [But] when women avoid conferences or are treated like second-class citizens at them, they lose out in their careers. Speaking at conferences is a great way to increase your network and reputation quickly. Conferences are good places to build working relationships with colleagues, and in some fields they are the only face-to-face networking opportunity. One way to patch up the leaky pipeline of women in tech is to make conferences more welcoming and exciting for women: not only reduce harassment, but come up with activities and perks that are more attractive to women."

Others are working on the issue as well. In London, the Articulate network is working to combat the argument that conference founders cannot find female speakers. Through a database of women speakers, courses in public speaking, and conference partnerships, the organization is trying to increase the number of women speaking at conferences. In other words, both men and women will have to work together throughout the STEM, entrepreneurship, and innovation industries to make sure that women are welcomed and treated as equals.

Overcoming Discrimination with Guts, Grit, and Goodwill

SUJATA SRINIVASAN

Sujata Srinivasan is an award-winning journalist for the WNPR News business desk. A full-time freelancer, her work has appeared in numerous publications, including Forbes.com, the Indian edition of Forbes, and multiple regional publications. Previously she was the interim chief of bureau at CNBC-TV 18 India and the editor of Connecticut Business Magazine.

I first met Bala Krishnamurthy at an event in Hartford, Connecticut, where she was honored for her professional success. She is the first woman to receive the coveted Engelberger Award for technology development—an Oscar equivalent in the robotics world—and is the founder of Aeolean Inc., which designs and develops software for robotic devices. I introduced myself as a business journalist, and we soon found we were from the same hometown. She then invited me over for a home-cooked meal. That was the start of what became a wonderful and close friendship.

When Krishnamurthy was ready to enter the workforce in 1979, hiring managers were skeptical of her abilities and her commitment—despite a master's in math. She'd never worked, and she had two small children, a fact that didn't go over well with her interviewer. "What would you do," he asked, "if a child is sick and you needed to go home?" She assured him that her parents, who lived nearby, would care for them during work hours.

Krishnamurthy then made a deal with him. "I said I'd come on board for about $15,000 a year and would prove myself in six months. If I failed, he could fire me. But if I succeeded, he'd have to compensate me well above that amount." And that's how she became the only woman in the engineering department at Unimation Inc.

"I was straightforward and outspoken, and men didn't like that," she said. "Many saw me as a bitch. But coming across as 'nice' never really crossed my mind." She ignored the innuendo-laced chatter, worked hard, set ambitious goals, and asked a lot of questions. For instance, why, when the highest raise was 10 percent, did she fall short at 9? What would she need to prove to become head of the software design team? She eventually got there, after getting a second master's in computer science. Through it all, she chose to overlook how people reacted to her, like the time in Japan when she was sent to train engineers on Unimation's control systems. "There I was in a room full of men, and the only women they were comfortable with were the ones serving them tea," she recalls. "They just didn't know how to treat a female colleague with respect."

But, said Krishnamurthy, she was lucky to have male mentors who were wonderfully good people. "There weren't any women high up in my industry at the time," she said. "So all my mentors were male, and they taught me valuable lessons." One of them was her boss, Joseph Engelberger, referred to as the father of robotics. Krishnamurthy recalls an incident when she'd spent all weekend, even canceling plans with her family, to work on a specific robot problem in the field. "Mr. Engelberger came in on Monday and asked the team where we were on the resolution. We had not resolved the issue, although we were close, but I told him about the effort our team had put in over the weekend," she said. "He promptly replied, 'The effort you put in may be important to you, but what matters to ME is the result.'" Years later, it was Engelberger who helped her get a consulting position in Paris so that she could be closer to her son, who was studying in Germany at the time.

In the case of Radha Jalan, the CEO of ElectroChem Inc., a fuel cell company in Massachusetts, the path to success was a lonely one with no mentors or even believers. Nobody expected Jalan to succeed when, at the age of 45, she took over from her husband, who had died of a heart attack. At the time, ElectroChem had zero receivables and three months worth of accounts payable, which Jalan paid from his life insurance money. With two children in school and bills mounting at home, she had to get a job quickly. The day of her husband's funeral, Jalan turned down a job offer from the state government, opting instead to run the company he'd founded. Her decision prompted all the top executives—but one—to resign.

"I had a PhD in education, but knew nothing about fuel cells or business. They believed I'd fail," she said. "My reasoning was: if I fail, that's fine. Nobody expects me to make it. But if I succeed, I will prove everyone wrong."

Over the next two years, Jalan fired the one remaining executive after she found him stealing from the company and took on a venture capital firm after she raised doubts about her own COO. The VC investor told her, "You're not a technical person, you don't have an MBA, you have no credibility. We invested in your company because of your COO. If you fire him, we'll take you to court and make sure you end up in the soup kitchen line."

Far from backing down, Jalan went ahead and fired her COO and hired two law firms, telling them that she couldn't afford a legal battle, but that they had to pretend otherwise by sending the VC a strongly worded letter, naming the COO as a third-party defendant. The matter was settled out of court in her favor.

"They thought I was a weak, single woman who could be easily intimidated," Jalan said. And it was her gender and ethnicity, she believes, that made the VC investor speak the way he did. After standing her ground, she went on to win NASA contracts, which became a turning point for her company.

Liddy Karter is the only female managing director at

Enhanced Capital Partners in Connecticut, an investment firm whose collaborators include Berkshire Hathaway and Vulcan Capital. She manages a portfolio of $70 million and invests her own money in Golden Seeds, a venture group focused on businesses founded by female entrepreneurs.

"There are benefits and costs to being an outlier of any kind," she said. "Being the minority gender in finance excludes me from valuable informal networking, and it was harder to find mentors and role models at the top of organizations. But on the other hand, it forced me to develop a broad base of connections since I didn't have a particular senior person who could assist me."

Karter found that gender discrimination at the senior levels of finance is so cordial, it's hard to discern. But she said it's certainly there as evidenced by the scarcity of female senior investment professionals in finance. In the private equity world, where so much value is placed on personal networks, this can impede access to information and deal flow.

"But women can wrest an advantage by developing networks that might be less available to their male peers: a parallel universe strategy," she explained. "Another useful technique is to interpret discrimination in a positive light. For instance, the next time your six foot four', square-jawed, broad-shouldered colleague restates what you just said and everyone nods approvingly after looking bored when you spoke, just thank him for agreeing with you. These patterns are so ingrained they probably don't realize they're overlooking you."

Some of the barriers for women can also come from other women, and Karter candidly explained how she overcame her own doubts. "I was hesitant to invest in businesses founded by women who have a lot of young children, and one woman had four," she confides. "But I'm glad I went ahead because it turned out to be a very good decision. My friend Agata Dulnik, PhD, a senior executive at Accenture's Capability Network, leading the company's Talent and Organization practice in Europe and the Middle East, said that at some point women will have to assess their own values to answer the question—is career important to me in the context of me as a mother? "If the answer is yes, then we have a responsibility to figure out how to best go after what we want and to be successful at it. Values, strategy, tactics."

She said pregnant women and women with small children often jump through hoops to get the job. "I remember when years back, I was a VP at a multinational technology company, we interviewed a young lady who was five months pregnant," she said. "The interviewing committee had a very—and passionately so—split line of recommendations: half of us were for hiring her and half against. Those that voted against reminded us of the time pressures that our project teams faced on a daily basis and speculated on how long this woman would choose to stay home with the baby once it was born. The other half of us just focused on her talents, energy, and the commitment to adding value she emphasized during her interviews. In the end, we ended up making her an offer. We never regretted it. She turned out to be such an asset to us—innovative, goal-oriented, and dedicated. She came back to work within the time agreed and eventually, through her efforts to give her very best to both her work and her baby, managed to warm up the hearts of the toughest and most experienced engineering managers we had in our organization."

CHAPTER 7
WOMEN CHANGING THE WORKPLACE

For the allocation of work in the technology and innovation industries to change, so must the workplaces. Despite the challenges facing women in technology, the gender wage gap is still smaller in STEM fields (14 percent) than other fields (21 percent).[44] Yet equality can be a very vague concept until the rubber meets the road of reality.

Are technology and innovation industries changing the culture of workplaces? And if so, how? We spoke with Megan Smith, an effusive speaker who had moderated an event highlighting Google's women technologists. She described her parents and her schooling as helping open her to choices to move into entrepreneurship and mechanical engineering, particularly around energy. But green energy research funding dried up, and she ended up doing her graduate work with tech/design pioneer Woodie Flowers at the MIT Media Lab. After that, she went to Apple in Tokyo and then came to Silicon Valley as an early team member at the pioneering, but ultimately too early and financially unsuccessful, company General Magic. The company has been nicknamed "the Fairchild of Mobile" because much of the top talent who created today's largest smartphone platforms were on that early team.

She then became the CEO of PlanetOut, a gay and lesbian online content and community company funded by AOL and others. She went from doing more technical work

---

[44] David Beede, Tiffany Julian, David Langdon, George McKittrick, Beethika Khan, and Mark Doms. "Women in STEM: A Gender Gap to Innovation." U.S. Department of Commerce. August 2011.

to more business development, saying, "I think mechanical engineering, and engineering in general, is great background for any work. Once I went to Google, I actually moved away from direct technology work into tech partnerships. I really am an entrepreneur type, so I move more into collaboration for innovation." Her work during her tenure included running Google's New Business Development team for eight years, where her team helped engineers and product managers across the company globally get new products launched, like Gmail, Book Search, Android, Chrome, and Google Translate. She also led the acquisition of companies, talent, and technologies for several products, including Google Earth and Google Maps. Recently joining the Google[x] team, she also created "Solve for X" with Astro Teller, a platform that brings together top tech talent to help accelerate "moonshot pioneers"—people with big ideas and nascent projects for solving huge problems in the world with technology innovations.

As a company, Google offers employees the chance to participate in affinity groups called ERGs, or Employee Research Groups. She is the executive liaison to Gayglers [LGBT], VetNet [Veterans], GAIN [Google American Indian Network], and a co-executive representative for the Women@Google. The upside for Google supporting these self-organized interest groups is that as the company expands, it seeks more talented employees via the group networks and works to help these employees thrive; it also seeks new markets and suppliers. The company has an internal research team called "PI Labs"—People Innovation Labs—whose broad range of work includes learning about how bias manifests in the workplace and the pipeline and creating company-wide trainings to share those learnings. For example, one study on employment finds that if a job description has ten criteria, men will apply, on average, when they have three of the job criteria; women will apply when they meet seven. That means that there might be people who are more qualified for the job and not raising their hand. Google, according to Smith, has also researched how to deal with a self-nomination process within the company. Men are more likely to self-nominate for promotions than women. Google held seminars for senior women urging and training them to self-nominate more and is looking into these processes overall.

Additionally, Google studied algorithms to assess where they were losing potential female employees. For example, they found women only interviewed by men were less likely to accept an offer. In an effort to retain employees, Google lengthened maternity leave to five months from three and from partial to full pay after discovering that attrition rates for postpartum women was twice that of other employees, and they also expanded paternity leave. To attract women and parents, the company also offers subsidized childcare, a $500 stipend for takeout meals after a baby is born, seven weeks of paid leave for new fathers, and dry cleaners onsite.[45]

Understanding the data behind how a workplace operates is, then, only the first part of the solution. Megan Smith strongly believes that the visibility of technical women, including historical context, could help today's entrepreneurs and innovators. "I think technical women are largely invisible both historically and currently. You [at *Innovating Women*] get to figure out how to get the lost history stories told and make the current women who are doing awesome work more visible."

Of course, there is an array of efforts to surface the history of female innovators, past and present. For example, in 2012, the Royal Society and Wikimedia UK teamed up to add Wikipedia entries on pioneering female scientists who hadn't been documented on that platform. Those added to the online platform included cognitive neuroscience professor Eleanor Maguire, who charted changes in brain structure as trainee London taxi drivers studied for three to four years to master a tremendously difficult exam about London roads known as "the knowledge."[46] The Google Doodle team finally moved birthday doodles to half men and half women, after discovering that their

---

[45] Claire Cain Miller, "In Google's Inner Circle, a Falling Number of Women," *The New York Times,* August 22, 2012.

[46] Maev Kennedy, "Forgotten Women of Science Win Recognition Online," *The Guardian,* October 19, 2012.

unconscious bias, coupled with biases in historical reporting, had caused them to celebrate almost no women's birthdays in doodles in the first seven years of the program.

"You're starting to see changes across the organizations," said Smith. "Because of unconscious bias training and company-wide goal-setting to improve in these areas, many Googlers have become much more aware of the problems and deep challenges as well as the actual value and importance of diversity, and they are taking action, asking for more research, and getting creative around solution pilots and programs."

Innovation is gaining momentum. Smith's colleague, Mary Grove, is the director of global entrepreneurship outreach at Google. Grove launched the company's Google for Entrepreneurs program, which has a strong international outreach to female entrepreneurs.

"In our three years since launch, we've worked with more than seventy partners with a mission of fostering entrepreneurship in local communities around the world (in more than one hundred countries) and pulling together technology and tools to equip entrepreneurs to be successful," she said. "Take, for example, our Online Learning Center, which provides free and open access to quality educational content. Another example of this is the recent Campus for Moms program, run out of our Campus Tel Aviv and Campus London spaces—they run a nine-week program for new moms and women on maternity leave, equipping them to launch startups." Google also works with organizations including Women 2.0 and Black Girls Code.

Within our discussion boards, the strongest call to action to create change was increased networking opportunities. The National Center for Women & Information Technology (NCWIT) is one of the largest organizations, with members of more than 450 prominent corporations, academic institutions, government agencies, and nonprofits focused on increasing women's participation in technology and computing across the pipeline with programs from elementary school through workforce participation.[47] Many companies have already started to embrace

[47] "NCWIT Fact Sheet," National Center for Women & Information Technology.

the need for women's networks. Catherine Rose, senior product manager at Philips, said companies should "set up and support women's leadership networks to help foster connectedness. My loyalty to my current company is supported by the women's network in place. It has allowed me many connections that my day job wouldn't have offered."

How Differences in Leadership Styles Are Explained Through Gender

SHAZIA SIDDIQI

Shazia Siddiqi is a technology professional at Fleetmatics in Rolling Meadows, Illinois. She received her MS and BS in computer science and math from Loyola University Chicago. Throughout her career, she has held various roles involving development, consulting, business systems analysis, project management, and process re-engineering.

I can still remember a conversation I had with a male coworker of mine much earlier on in my career. Our manager was a woman who was very particular about the processes we had to follow and the documentation we had to create for any of the projects we were working on. The mandate came from the CIO, and she made sure that her team followed the framework set forth. In our team meetings, I recall my coworker getting into fiery debates with our manager about how to manage risks for our projects and whether or not following the procedures set by the organization was critical or, as he thought, overkill. After one such heated meeting, he came to me to vent. He said that this is why he hates working for female managers. He went on to say that he had never had a good experience working with female leaders, and that he thought they always felt the need to prove themselves and were unnecessarily demanding of their subordinates—especially the male ones. I was taken aback by the conversation. First of all, I thought it was odd that he was openly telling me, a woman, about how he felt regarding female leaders. I also then had to ask myself whether or not I thought there was any truth to what he was saying. I had no issues with our manager, nor did the other three members of our gender-mixed team. We understood the need to follow the procedures set in place in order to reduce operational risk to the organization. So why did my coworker feel this way? Would he have been so opposed to following the procedures had the direction come from a male manager? And more importantly, why did he immediately attribute his differences in opinions with our manager to a gender issue?

Since then, throughout my various roles and career changes, I've worked with many other male and female leaders. In fact, I've even managed small teams myself. What I've observed is that, just like their male counterparts, female leaders have an array of varying leadership styles and approaches. I've worked with women who like to micromanage their staff and some who ask that you only come to them with issues. Some aren't in tune with what their team is working on, some follow a methodology to a tee, some work on building a rapport with their team, and some don't want you to speak to them until spoken to (I work the least effectively with that management style!).

However, what has been a reoccurring theme in my experience is that whenever there's conflict between a female manager and a team member, her gender is almost always the first thing that's pointed out. Very rarely do I notice gender coming up when a team member doesn't get along with a male manager. If I were to have a conversation again with that male coworker of mine from so long ago, I would challenge him to question why our manager's gender was so easily brought up. I would ask him whether or not he'd feel comfortable with someone using his gender, race, religion, age, or background to justify differing opinions with his management approach. I know I wouldn't.

Changing the Game

The big question is: what does it take to change a workplace? First, commitment to the goal. Second, a willingness to do a deep self-assessment. And third, the implementation and ongoing reevaluation of strategies to make sure they work. Analyst and investor Esther Dyson also points to a difference between the diversity strategies of startups, which often are formed through friend-circles and of companies that are scaling much larger. "Candidly, startups are just struggling to stay alive, so diversity is rarely on their agenda, and they don't have enough people to *be* genuinely diverse. The small ones especially just tend to cofound with or hire their dormmates. Once they've reached some size, ideally they start to think about building a team of the best rather than of the familiar." Corporations who have gone to scale have implemented a variety of programs, including the Hacker School/Etsy partnership; Cisco's Inclusive Advocacy Program, a nine-month mentorship with an executive that helps build employee connections; and the Yahoo! Women In Tech Employee Resource Group, which includes travel funding for conferences and partnering with organizations, such as the Anita Borg Institute for Women, that focus on women in tech.[48] Of course, the numbers of women vary widely in different parts of the technology sectors. Bright Labs released data about the percentage of men in each of the following jobs and found:

> *92.7 percent of network engineers are men; 92.6 percent of desktop support technicians; 91.6 percent of network administrators; 91.6 percent of network technicians;*

---

[48] "Companies Leading the Way: Putting the Principles into Practice," United Nations Global Compact, March 2012.

91.5 percent of PC technicians; 90.8 percent of computer technicians; 90.4 percent of IT support; 89.7 percent of system administrators; 89.7 percent of systems administrators; 89.5 percent of senior software developers; 88.6 percent of application engineers; 79.8 percent of database administrators; 78.3 percent of software engineers; 78.1 percent of software developers; 77.8 percent of technical support specialists; 77.1 percent of programmers; 77.1 percent of web developers; 77.1 percent of senior software engineers; 76.7 percent of developers; 75 percent of senior programming analysts; 72.3 percent of systems analysts; 68.4 percent of help desk analysts; 67.8 percent of programming analysts; 66 percent of web designers; 66 percent of software test engineers; 65 percent of IT project managers; 63.7 percent of application developers; 53.8 percent of data analysts.[49]

In addition, a 2012 survey by McKinsey & Company titled "Unlocking the Full Potential of Women at Work" highlighted some of the broader issues facing women. In a survey of sixty companies, most of them Fortune 500 corporations, McKinsey found key levers that helped push a more gender-diverse workforce. Few companies utilized them all. The report states that researchers "found twelve companies among the sixty surveyed that met at least three of these standards":

1. A starting position that reflects the talent. We set the bar at the Fortune 500 average share of women accounting for 53 percent (or more) of entry-level professionals or at women having the same odds of advancing to the manager level as men; thirty-one companies met or exceeded this cutoff.

2. Better odds of promotion. Based on figures from the top third of participants, we identified companies in which women's chances for advancing from manager to director and then to vice president were at least

---

[49] Jacob Bollinger, "The Tech Gender Gap: Title Analysis," Bright.com, May 24, 2013.

85 percent of men's chances for doing so; twenty companies met or exceeded this metric.

3.   More women at the top. Based on figures from the top third of participants, we set this metric as having at least 22 percent female representation on the executive committee; nineteen companies met this bar.

4.   Women in the line. Finally, again based on figures from the top third of participants, we looked for companies with at least 55 percent of women vice presidents and senior vice presidents in line positions; twenty companies made this cut.

The report continues, "Almost every participant achieved one of these metrics—in fact, fifty-two companies did. About half of the participants achieved two—twenty-seven companies did. We raised the bar to three of the four conditions, and twelve companies rose to the top. They outperformed the pool's average by a significant margin, especially at the highest levels of leadership. Small improvements along the pipeline really do make the difference."[50]

[50] Joanna Barsh and Lareina Yee, "Unlocking the Full Potential of Women at Work," McKinsey & Company, 2012.

Why Female Managers Need to Take the Lead

CARRIE-ANNE MOSLEY

Carrie-Anne Mosley is head of global sales for BMC Software's Remedyforce, a solution built on the Salesforce.com platform. She is a cloud evangelist who speaks regularly on the benefits that cloud technologies can bring to companies and government agencies. Previously Carrie-Anne was a regional vice president at Salesforce. com with responsibilities over State and Local East as well as regional vice president for Enterprise Sales in the Mid-Atlantic States. Prior to Salesforce.com, she spent fourteen years at Oracle as a regional manager. Carrie-Anne has an MS in information systems and telecommunications from Johns Hopkins University and a BA in government and politics from the University of Maryland. Outside of work, Carrie-Anne enjoys spending time with her husband, young daughter, and their three dogs. She and her family are proud to support the Children's Science Center, an interactive children's museum being planned for Northern Virginia focused on science, technology, engineering, and math (www.childsci.org).

I never was a pageant girl—I made fun of a friend who was in the Miss Maryland pageant when we were in our early twenties. Yet for some reason, each year I'm drawn to watch the Miss USA pageant on television. I cheer for the representative from my state in hopes that she'll make it to the finals, as though she were a neighbor. Now in my forties, I see the pageant and the young women and think that my daughter could be standing in their shoes in a few years. They're all not only beautiful, but also charitable and smart. That's why last year I felt a pain in my stomach when Miss Utah stumbled horribly over her question during the final moments of the competition. The question posed by the judge asked why women, who are the primary income earners in 40 percent of U.S. households, are not paid at the same level as their male counterparts. Unfortunately, overcome by fear, Miss Utah was not able to convey her true feelings on the subject. After some thought, however, I am.

From the earliest time, we teach little girls to be polite, be quiet, and use good manners. These are generally good virtues, but as our young women age, we tell them to wait for a boy to ask them out, to be the cheerleaders, not to be too pushy, and that a pleasant appearance is necessary to have success in life and love. We culminate this by telling our young daughters that their love lives will only be complete when Prince Charming asks for their hands in marriage. Years later, we're finding ourselves in a place where we bring home the bacon and then are expected to fry it up in a pan, wash the pan, get the kids to bed so we can have rushed sex before falling asleep, and then do it all over again the next day. What is wrong with this picture?

I think pay equality starts in two places: at home with how we raise our daughters and at work with how we act as managers.

First, we need to teach our daughters that they have to communicate their wants and needs in life. If you want to spend time with a male, ask him. If your relationship isn't giving you what you want, tell him. I hope that I'm raising my daughter to be a confident woman. I don't believe that abandoning tradition is something that needs to be done to an extreme, but if she wants to marry a specific man, she should be able to communicate that to him and drive the action instead of waiting for him to "pop the question." The man doesn't always need to be in the relationship driver's seat, and it's important for our daughters to realize that.

Our daughters also need to understand that if they're not getting what they deserve in terms of compensation in the workplace, they need to speak up and ask for a raise. Often we think that men (at work and at home) can read our minds or will do what is right, but frankly they can't read minds and don't always realize when something's wrong. Women need to have confidence that they are adding value to the workplace and speak up for themselves in a constructive way.

As female managers, we need to treat all employees with parity regardless of sex. That said, we must recognize that sometimes giving people a break will lead them to success they never imagined. I once hired an entry-level technical consultant. She was the daughter of immigrants and was the first "success story" for her family. She went to college, and I hired her at one of the top technology companies. At the same time, her younger sister had dropped out of school and had a child out of wedlock. It didn't take me long to realize that this new employee needed a strong mentor to help her see the path to success. However, what I couldn't give her was self-confidence.

During her first year on the job, she tried to resign two or three times. Each time, I rejected her resignation and pushed her to keep with it. I believe a man would have let her give up. She went on to have an amazing career for more than ten years at that company before leaving last year to start a family. I would hire her again in a moment if she ever gives me that opportunity.

Last year, I had the opportunity to hire a former colleague who had been out of the technology community for almost eight years raising a family. A lot of people questioned my hiring decision, but I had confidence that this woman had not lost her edge. While raising her family, she successfully started her own real estate business. Selling houses is not quite the same as selling enterprise software, but that risk was one I took without hesitation. The gamble paid off, and that employee is now a top performer.

As female managers, we can help solve the challenge of equal pay for equal work by recognizing the inequality and demanding action. We can hire employees with fair pay, we can allow moms to reenter the workforce at competitive pay levels for the current market, and we can support young women as they enter the working world. We can mentor and advise them on how to negotiate their compensation so that they position themselves fairly for long-term employment and advancement within their companies.

Is this an easy problem to solve? No. But with women rising up in the ranks of corporate America, we have an opportunity to work to fix the problem. I am optimistic that as leaders in the technology industry today, we are setting a great example for young women. We must continue to encourage their pursuit of STEM careers, show them the path to financial success, and help them in asking for the job and salary that they want.

Finding the Fit

Among the women in our forums, there was a wide-ranging discussion of how to evaluate workplace policies and the limitations of each situation. For example, Anne Neville, director of the State Broadband Initiative at the U.S. Department of Commerce, said of virtual employment, "I think it really depends on the company/role/project and how 'virtual' virtual is. I now work remotely, but I couldn't do it if I hadn't spent the first two and a half years of the project in the office (usually for twelve-hours a day). This created the relationships so that I'm not the strange voice on the phone or face on video. However, in previous organizations set up with people in different time zones, some working independently and some in small groups, initial face time wasn't required to build the relationships."

And some of our participants offered advice for men and women in power. Maura Daly Adamcyzk, former senior manager at Palladium Energy, which manufactures custom lithium ion battery packs, said, "Quit assigning females the paperwork, scheduling, and 'soft' people work on your team. Unless women get real experience early in their career in the technical 'trenches,' they will not have the opportunity to gain respect and visibility like their male counterparts. Think past gender in assigning work and forming teams. Don't judge all women from one experience with a female technical worker. Women are as individual as men."

Priscilla Oppenheimer, an independent consultant in the computer networking field, learned that keeping an eye on job options is key. "The worst piece of advice I got was to stay put in a job, despite it being a dead end. My colleague told me to 'keep your head down, do a good job, and you'll be golden.' This colleague didn't really care if I succeeded. He liked having me around because I was friendly, but he didn't care about my career aspirations. Also, he was suggesting a strategy that worked for him and not considering what might work for me. I stayed at the job for five years and was unable to succeed, mostly because the men in the all-male group were misogynists. The man who gave me the advice was the nicest of the men in the group, but even he had a tendency to call any strong woman who expressed her opinions 'a bitch.' I should have recognized that this workplace was toxic and not stayed five years!"

In fact, more and more studies are showing how deeply a bad job fit can affect our physical and mental health. A 2013 study by the Finnish Institute of Occupational Health found that job stress was a risk factor for diabetes—and that risk was higher for women than men in similar circumstances.[51] And the American Psychological Association added, "Burnout can lead to depression, which, in turn, has been linked to a variety of other health concerns, such as heart disease and stroke, obesity and eating disorders, diabetes, and some forms of cancer. Chronic depression also reduces your immunity to other types of illnesses and can even contribute to premature death."[52] Gender-bias is just one of many sources of stress for working women, and each woman has to take her own health seriously and know if and when it's time to walk away from a once-promising job.

In order to change workplaces, pioneers must be willing to enter previously heavily or all-male sectors of the industry. Laina Greene is executive director and chief strategy and investment officer for IBS Tower, a publicly traded telecommunications network in Indonesia. After spending fourteen years in the Bay Area, Greene took an executive position at the company. "Indonesia today is one of the fastest growing countries in the

[51] S.T. Nyberg, E.I. Fransson, K. Heikkilä, L. Alfredsson, A. Casini, et al. "Job Strain and Cardiovascular Disease Risk Factors: Meta-analysis of Individual-participant Data from 47,000 Men and Women. *PLoS ONE* 8(6): e67323. (2013) doi:10.1371/journal.pone.0067323

[52] "Mind/Body Health: Job Stress," American Psychological Association, http://www.apa.org/helpcenter/job-stress.aspx.

region, and so I decided to grab the opportunity to be a part of the Asian century. I also serve on a steering committee of an informal investment fund that invest into new disruptive technology companies, such as mobile payments and data visualization. There is so much room for innovation in a country of 240 million people with more than 240 million mobile phone subscriptions."

Indonesian tech is male-dominated, judging by Greene's descriptions. She has been breaking barriers throughout her career—and has a great role model. "My mother herself was a pioneer as an Indian woman who managed to get a degree in physics. She came from humble beginnings in India and was told a woman cannot do science. She not only studied science, but topped her university. However, when she came to Singapore, her degree was not recognized, so she went back to the university in Singapore and got her second degree and her master's degree in physics. When I started off in telecom back in 1986, I was one of the few female professionals at these international conferences. Men would harass me or just ignore me and if not for the backing of my boss and his boss, it would have been very hard for me to make it. They not only supported me, but promoted my work, helping me be recognized as an expert in this industry. After twenty-five years in this industry, I still think it is a very male-dominated world. Women still struggle to be heard and be taken seriously. I think key to the solution also lies with men who are forward-thinking, who promote women and will promote the next generation of women, too."

It can be frustrating to face the obvious bias that occurs even once you have secured a key position. Greene said, "I had a very interesting incident last year at an event at Stanford University. There was a speaker talking about smart grids, something I was very interested in and had learned a lot about. I put up my hand to ask questions, but he would only ask the people in front of me, behind me, or even next to me. So after the class, I went up to ask him why he would not allow me to ask my question and he said with surprise, 'Oh sorry, I did not see you.' He did seem genuinely surprised. Another Stanford educator told me that that was her experience usually at campus, too (but then she and I are both non-Caucasian, so it's hard to tell if it is a women issue or a race issue). So even in the United States, we still have a long way to go in terms of removing these inherent prejudices."

For other women, reshaping the workplace comes in the form of launching their own businesses. Darlene Damm is the cofounder of DIYROCKETS, which uses an open-source approach to lowering the costs of space technology. Over the years, she learned to trust her own intuition when it came to innovating. "Women are encouraged to pay attention to what other people think and how other people judge them and their ideas. You have to think for yourself and decide for yourself and then test your idea in the marketplace and then respond to that. And then you have to train your own imagination to see who you are and what you can do in the world in a larger way. Initially this can be a lonely process, but once you figure it out, it is very powerful." She added, "I know that over the course of my career and in my life I've been underpaid, undervalued, and overlooked multiple times because of my gender. On the other hand, I think I have also had people and institutions support me specifically because they want to help women succeed. The most important thing is to learn to quickly identify people or institutions that do not respect women and stay away from them, no matter how good they might be in other aspects."

As we survey how companies treat women in the fields of STEM, we see a variety of outcomes, from bias to opportunity, based on factors including national and regional culture, corporate culture, and the age and stage of a company. (Early-stage startups tend to focus less, at least in a structured way, on fostering diversity than more mature companies.) The bottom line for women in the field is that each person has to make her own decision about how to navigate the inevitable pitfalls of any workplace, when and if to decide enough is enough, and of course, how to make the company and field better not just for herself, but for others.

CHAPTER 8
WOMEN AFFECTING FUNDING

In 1973, fresh out of college and with a double major in business and math, Ann Winblad started as a systems analyst at the Federal Reserve Bank of Minneapolis. Despite concerns about her student loans, after thirteen months she decided her current environment lacked the challenges that she needed to thrive. "My dad was a high school basketball coach, so we were always doing competitions. Who could run around the yard fastest. We each had our own little personal stopwatches," she explained. "Unfortunately, my energy level is quite a bit different than the people at the bank." Her solution: "I just resigned one day. I decided, 'I'm just going to write my resignation letter and just start my own company.'" This, plus a $500 loan from her brother, was the start of Open Systems Incorporated, a financial and accounting software firm.

Believing in her ability to write software, she convinced three friends to go on sabbatical or quit their jobs and join her. First they won the proposal for the Student Accounting System for the state of Minnesota, which provided base funding. The team designed the school system software during the day and their own at night, negotiating free access to the computers of a local computer reseller in the evenings. Unfortunately, the reseller lacked evening air conditioning. "If you're in Minneapolis today," she said while speaking to us one summer day, "it's about a hundred degrees. And my three guys decided that the best way to stay cool was just to strip all their clothes off. And unfortunately, the office manager came in that night, and she really didn't understand this whole naked programming concept, so we were banned from using their computers." Winblad was faced with a new dilemma: raising money to buy computers.

Making a list of all the banks in Minneapolis and St. Paul, Winblad set out to raise capital. After receiving eight prompt "No's," she stood on the steps of the ninth and last bank and decided to switch up her strategy. "I could know exactly when they were going to say 'No,' so at home I'd practice crying in front of a mirror. So, when the guy would start saying 'No,' I would burst into tears. And the last bank, when I did that, he goes, 'We'll just take care of you, just stop crying.' And they loaned us the $25,000 we needed for all those computers."

She read her audience and gave them what they wanted: vulnerability. It was a strategy some would consider controversial, but it worked. Next, she needed skilled employees for cheap. For their first programmers, she negotiated, saying, "How much do you spend on food per month?" Based on their response, she would offer to pay for all their food if she could deduct that sum from their salary. She said, "I'd already figured out how to qualify anyone for food stamps in the state of Minnesota. So, for a year, we hired our programmers with a package that was salary and food stamps." Again, Winblad wasn't afraid of unusual methods to make her company viable.

Six years after its founding, Open Systems sold for $15 million, thirty thousand times Winblad's original $500 investment. From Winblad's story, the level of creativity and tenacity necessary for an entrepreneur to be successful is clear. A startup team needs to want it so badly that they are willing to go the extra distance 24/7 for as long as it takes. In this case, it involved some unusual and even controversial methods— coding without air conditioning (or clothes) and crying in front of potential investors.

During the seventies, when Winblad founded Open Systems, software companies were a new concept. Apple and Oracle were just two of the pioneering tech companies founded during that decade. Today, the market is more established and saturated, causing investors to have assumptions about who fits their idea of an entrepreneur. Although entrepreneurs can prosper from a more streamlined process, it can also lead to biases toward those who do not fit the typical mold: a preconceived profile of education, background, gender, race, and/or class. Babson's 2012 Global Entrepreneurship Monitor report found the median capital of male entrepreneurs is $30,000, relative to female entrepreneurs, whose median is less than $8,000.[53] There are serious barriers that women face when applying for various types of capital—deficits in technical knowledge, connections to financial networks, and an overall lack of confidence.

One consistency since the seventies is the benefit of a STEM background when raising funds. According to Heidi Roizen, the operating partner at Draper Fisher Jurvetson, most venture capitalists are attracted to companies where there is the opportunity to dominate a market. Today, startups often have very technical underpinnings because this creates a barrier to entry for competitors. Loretta McCarthy, managing director of Golden Seeds, said, "Many of the companies that we see have some sort of technology as a core part of their solution. So the more women who have working knowledge of technology, the more we will see." Here the overlap of how a lack of women in the fields of STEM creates a deficit of female entrepreneurs is clear. Oftentimes women enter STEM fields later on in life, again creating a different background than many of the men with whom they are competing for funds. It is not only lack of access to capital sources that is barring women from funding, but also the lack of female investors.

From the Center for Venture Research, "In 2005, women represented 8.7 percent of all angel investors; as of 2012, this number has grown to 21.8 percent." And in 2011, only 12 percent of venture capitalists were women.[54] Only 22 percent of U.S. startups have one or more women on their funding teams.[55] And a 2012 study found that women are almost twice as likely to

[53] Donna J. Kelley, Candida G. Brush, Patricia G. Greene and Yana Litovsky. "Global Entrepreneurship Monitor: 2012 Women's Report." Babson College. 2013.

[54] Jeffrey Sohl, "The Angel Investor Market in 2012: A Moderating Recovery Continues," Center for Venture Research, April 25, 2013.

[55] "Startup Outlook: 2013 Report," Silicon Valley Bank, 2013.

discontinue their business due to an inability to secure funding. Difficulty in financing is the most often cited reason women in the United States discontinue their business (25 percent cite this reason, compared with 14 percent of men).[56] According to Deborah Jackson, cofounder of the Women Innovate Mobile (WIM) Accelerator and a member of Golden Seeds with more than twenty years of experience in raising capital, this lack of women on the investment side has hurt women's access to capital. "If you really look at how money is allocated and given to early-stage companies, it starts with who has the money," she said. "The fact of the matter is that men control the flow of capital to early-stage companies."

Funding entrepreneurial efforts through venture capital and getting access to larger scale investments have been the greatest pitfalls for women who, without access to this network, lose access to investors. The investment process, at its core, is about belief—belief in the vision of the founder, belief the founder will prevail and solve unforeseen challenges, belief that the founder will build and grow the company no matter what it takes, and belief that the idea can turn into a competitive and profitable company. "Men pick up the phone to open a door for one of their buddies," added Jackson. "If you have a door opened or you are part of a club, you get opportunities that someone from the outside has a hard time getting."

Women have tried to overcome this through investment organizations focused on women and ones that seek to connect women-led firms to capital, such as WIM, Golden Seeds, Belle Capital, Phenomenal, Women's Capital Fund, 37 Angels, and Women 2.0, to name a few. These programs are a great starting point to build women's access. But women's groups cannot, and should not, be the only sources of capital open to promising female-founded companies.

Oftentimes funding capital also comes with access to the

[56] Donna J. Kelley, Abdul Ali, Edward J. Rogoff, Candida Brush, Andrew Corbett, Mahdi Majbouri, Diana Hechavarria. "Global Entrepreneurship Monitor: 2012 United States Report." Babson College and Baruch College. 2012.

necessary network that will help a startup grow. McCarthy spoke about how Golden Seeds helps companies not only raise capital, but expand the relationships of early-stage firms: "These entrepreneurs frequently really struggle with opening doors in various corporations that they would like to call upon to sell their service or product. So we put a lot of thought into how we can be helpful after we have made the investment. This might include just using some of our members to help them think about their business plan. We also frequently think about what are the introductions that this company should have now."

This lack of network goes deeper than snagging an initial pitch. It expands to receiving advice for the development of a business strategy and introductions to help obtain clients.

How an Investment Banker Achieved Success as an Entrepreneur

DEBORAH JACKSON

Deborah Buresh Jackson is the founder and CEO of Plum Alley, a site for women to raise money for ventures. She founded Plum Alley in 2012 to provide new ways for women to access capital through the use of technology and their networks. Prior to that, she was an investment banker for more than two decades, and her clients included many health care technology and Internet companies. She was a founder of the Women Innovate Mobile Accelerator and has invested in many early-stage technology-related companies.

I grew up in a large family with four siblings and moved constantly during my youth. I was often thrown into new environments and new public schools and had to find my way. I went to a state college with subsidized tuition so that I could pay for my education, and I was the first in my family to get a college diploma and a graduate degree. After my undergraduate years in Michigan, I moved to Boston with a box of possessions and fifty dollars in my pocket. I lived in the dining room of a friend's apartment, worked in a Chinese restaurant in Cambridge, and found my first professional job through the newspaper job ads. All of this instilled a sense of self-reliance, taught me to deal with uncertainty, and honed my survival instinct, but I didn't have any contacts or role models to turn to. So I just closed my eyes and asked, "What do I want my life to be like? How will I get there?"

Like other women, I worked because I had to. I decided that I wanted to make enough money in my career to provide for my family and give them more opportunities. After Columbia Business School in 1980, I joined Goldman Sachs. The technology industry did not have a presence in New York in any meaningful way at the time, so I was not exposed to tech as a career option. As an investment banker, my first clients were nonprofits and hospitals, and later health care technology and Internet companies.

Wall Street was, and is, a brutal environment for women. Women are in the minority, particularly in C-level positions. The inequality in pay, promotion, and recognition hurts the soul and spirit. After twenty-one years, I hung up my boxing gloves and, with a great sense of relief, left Wall Street. I then coached female entrepreneurs because they were the happiest women I had met. They had dreams, they were using and building technology—they were creating their own destinies. Looking to them, I decided to get back in the game in a new way with my own rules, and I founded a company.

Why did I become an entrepreneur? Because I wanted to have a big impact, and I knew I would find a way to do that. As women, we must build our companies, our networks, and our wealth. We have no other choice. The only way to be optimistic about the future is to change things when you see something that isn't right or is unfair.

I am keenly aware that women need access to capital and the right advisors to open doors for them, so I founded my company, Plum Alley, and cofounded the WIM Accelerator, to provide the tools and connections to spur female entrepreneurs to success. I want to be an example for others that strong convictions matter, that you can found a company at any age, and that you can build an economically viable company that matters.

With that in mind, there are three things I think are necessary for success: absolute conviction, the need to succeed, and money.

Absolute conviction means no half-ways, no equivocation. What you are doing is not optional. You care so deeply that you will never give up. You have profound determination because you care that much. What you are doing matters.

The second factor is that you have no choice but to succeed, and you will do what it takes to get there. You ignore all the naysayers and surround yourself with people who believe in you and your idea. You will not back down. You will succeed and you will make something out of nothing because you have to. You must survive, and you must make that contribution to the world.

The final ingredient is the money to build your dream. The best way to build and grow a business is with the income you generate in your company—build a product that someone wants so much they will pay big bucks for it. And when you need outside capital, go for it. There are so many parallels between Wall Street and venture capital firms. Both investment banking firms and venture capital firms are about allocating capital, and both are dominated by white men and operate as a club.

So what do you do? Walk out of any meeting where the investor doesn't get what you are doing and don't look back. Remind yourself that venture investors are not gods. In fact, the returns on most VC portfolios are lower than the market in general.

VCs need you to make returns. If they don't get it, just move on and prove them wrong. You will survive because you have to. Close your eyes and say, "What do I want my life to be like? How will I get there?"

The Confidence to Lead

As we will see, the overt sexism of the past has decreased, but more subtle stereotypes about female entrepreneurs' abilities to build their businesses persist. Many women on our discussion boards mentioned the discrimination they faced in their attempts to raise capital. Lori Skagen Mehen, founder and CMO at Medlio, a company that provides virtual insurance identification cards, mentioned her fundraising horror story. Mehen, along with her two male partners, applied for a few accelerator programs for initial startup funding. They presented themselves to ten men and one woman on a panel. Her cofounders went first, speaking about their interests and their families, one having two children, the other three. Mehen followed suit, mentioning her interests and family, only to be asked by the men on the panel: "What makes you think, as a mother, that you could possibly participate in this program?"

Mehen reflects on the experience: "I was absolutely stunned. Being a parent evidently presented no problem if you were a man, but was a big problem if you were a woman. Fortunately, before I could pick my jaw up off the floor, the one woman in the room chastised the men for their comment and the meeting continued." Luckily her team was accepted into a program that provided a limited amount of funding and access to resources and relationships that proved invaluable to her firm.

As Mehen points out, women on the investment side not only aid in women's network to access capital, but also cut through the biases in the room. The men did not consciously realize the different treatment of Mehen and her partners, and yet, without the female investor to point this out, may have not backed funding because of this issue.

McCarthy, of Golden Seeds, found that since women are less common applicants than men and thus less familiar to the investment audience, they have an extra hurdle in proving their leadership abilities: "Women are particularly scrutinized about leadership, so I do think that a lot of those attributes become particularly meaningful for women to exude—that they are capable leaders, they're capable of attracting great talent. They need to project confidence. They cannot have self-doubt about whether this is going to be a great company. Many women have been acculturated and socialized to have a certain amount of doubt—to not be too brash and too bold and too overconfident. Well, investors do want to see confidence. So the question is, what's the right mix?"

This issue of how women represent themselves came up repeatedly in our research. There has been much emphasis on how women appear less confident, but are social norms making women ill-prepared to cope with difficult situations? Lynn Tilton, the founder and CEO of Patriarch Partners explained: "Men are sort of raised to fight, right? Men are raised to be strong. I think women see strength sometimes as being able to deprive themselves to give to others, to be able to protect their young, to be able to put themselves last. But strength in terms of having to fight litigation, to have to fire people, to have to demand of people, I think it's just we haven't had—we've just not been inculcated to live that way."

But a lack of confidence or even a personal style that to a funder appears to lack confidence can make an entrepreneur fall short in their pitch. Today, more than even before, the ability to raise capital quickly is critical for success. Technology has decreased the cost of building a company, making the speed of market entry to dominating a market even more crucial. Linda Hayes, the founder of three software companies, including AutoTester, the first PC-based test automation tool, shared her experience in raising capital for her three firms. With the first, she raised $4 million in venture capital. In the second, having differences with the VC, she avoided raising funds this way: "Big mistake! A competitor with inferior technology raised a lot of money and ended up owning the market and selling for $5 billion while we went out of business. Ouch." Although not based on hesitation, Hayes gives an example on the importance of speed.

Mark Suster, an American entrepreneur, angel investor, and investment partner at GRP Partners, emphasizes this point in "A 6-Step Relationship Guide to VC": "If you wait until you're 'ready' to fund, you're too late. Funding is about developing a relationship over time. Most of us wouldn't get married on the first weekend we met someone in Vegas." Tilton refers to it in another way: "What I always say is, 'perfection, procrastination, paralysis,' is the circle of loss. You have to be able to make a decision, and drive it, and follow it, and then if it's not working, change it." Any hesitation, any questioning of oneself, can be detrimental to entrepreneurs.

It's not only about selling your idea; it's about selling yourself. "What you should really be focused on when pitching your early-stage startup is pitching yourself and your team," advises Chris Dixon, an American Internet entrepreneur and investor and cofounder, and former CEO of the website Hunch, in his article "Pitch Yourself, Not Your Idea." "The story you should tell is the story of someone who has been building stuff her whole life and now just needs some capital to take it to the next level."

According to the 2011 Global Entrepreneurship Monitor report, young men in the first half of their career have higher perceptions of opportunity, higher confidence in their capabilities, are less inhibited by a fear of failure, and are more likely to know an entrepreneur than women of the same age and the general population at older ages. The study found less than half of women feel they are capable of starting a business, while two-thirds of men do.[57] Joséphine de Chazournes, senior analyst at Celent, has also seen this lack of confidence in women: "The gender issue in raising money is not a big issue, I think. It is the more general entrepreneurship mentality that lacks in

---

[57] Donna J. Kelley, Abdul Ali, Edward J. Rogoff, Candida Brush, Andrew Corbett, Mahdi Majbouri, Diana Hechavarria. "Global Entrepreneurship Monitor: 2011 United States Report." Babson College and Baruch College. 2012.

women that should be tackled; if you want to go out there and get them, then you can go raise money; if you don't, of course you won't feel secure asking for money."

To prove her commitment to her company, Tilton put all of her savings on the table, including her daughter's college tuition fund. Unfortunately, our research found that many women do not show this level of confidence when pitching their product. For Aparna Vedapuri Singh, a founder-editor at Women's Web, this is one of the greatest issues women have in raising capital and the reason she decided to participate in the *Innovating Women* project: "While most men are gung-ho about their ideas (even if the idea is the nth clone of Facebook or Flickr or yet another e-commerce site with little differentiation), women are so diffident and hesitant to promote themselves and their ideas, and I include myself as one person having that problem."

The pitch is the representation of the skills of the leadership team for the future. McCarthy mentioned how in a small business, everyone has to be involved in sales: "So if the founder's a woman, you say, 'All right, this person has to walk into IBM, American Express, Bank of America, or Google, and convince them that they should try this product or service.' That's true with any of these companies, even if it's led by a man. But the chances are, when they go calling in on these companies, they're going to be calling on men. So you try to say, 'All right, how is that going to work? Can she pull it off?' Because ultimately, she is going to have to be successful at bringing in business." The pitch has to demonstrate the founder has the skills and commitment to succeed even if she is the only woman in a market dominated by men.

Our ambassadors had some tips for women trying to fight for funds. Hayes suggests: "Don't even think about the gender issue; it won't be an issue to the right investors, and if it is an issue, they are the wrong ones." Agustina Sartori, a telematics engineer and cofounder/director at GlamST, believes being one of the few women in the room can also help you stand out: "I think that gender has definitely affected our raising of funds in a positive way. I am a female engineer, young (twenty-six years old), and many times not identified as one by my looks and attitude—

which doesn't match with the prejudgment of what men and women think that a female engineer 'must' look like. This has always been a good approach because many times we have raised interest in our company because of us, seen as an exception and therefore an interesting story to hear. Also this raises doubts and confusion many times, and it depends on us turning this doubt into opportunities." When at a tech event in Uruguay, she met a key investor who at first said, "I don't think I really have much to talk to you about because I'm a techie nerd," but was then impressed and intrigued to hear Sartori was an engineer. He later invested in their firm, which Sartori attributes partially to their unique story as female tech entrepreneurs. "The approach is different because we are different," Sartori said. "When raising funds as women, we approach VCs involving feelings and passion in a different way. I feel they see us differently, but because we are different." Being a woman helped Sartori differentiate herself from the pack. Although some were confused by her image, with confidence she was able to control the conversation and shift it to focusing on her business and her potential.

Despite these setbacks, women-led businesses are on the rise. In 2012, 16 percent of those seeking angel investing were women. 25 percent of women-owned ventures seeking angel capital received funding compared to 20 percent of non-women-owned ventures, although this does not represent the total amount of funding received.[58] As of 2013, women-owned firms make up 29 percent of all U.S. firms, 30 percent of privately held firms, and up to 46 percent when including equally owned businesses. From 1997 to 2013, the number of businesses in the United States increased by 41 percent, while women-owned firms increased at 1.5 times the national average at 59 percent. As of 2013, it was estimated that there were 8.6 million women-owned businesses in the United States, generating $1.3 trillion in

[58]Jeffrey Sohl, "The Angel Investor Market in 2012: A Moderating Recovery Continues," Center for Venture Research, April 25, 2013, http://paulcollege.unh.edu/center-venture-research.

revenues and employing close to 7.8 million.[59]

The crowdfunding movement is also positively impacting women's access to capital. In 2012, crowdfunding platforms fetched $2.7 billion globally, an 81 percent increase over 2011.[60] According to Chance Barnett, cofounder of Crowdfunder, a global social and crowdfunding network for equity and contribution for small businesses, startups, and social enterprises, in an interview for Entrepreneur.com: "Not only are women more active on social media, they are often more collaborative when they do invest, so [crowdfunding] is going to be a really interesting space, and it is going to be the perfect place for women to gain a lot of traction."[61]

With resilience and persistence, no obstacle is too great. Winblad recalls her thoughts after receiving eight rejections: "By the time I was down to that ninth bank, it was like, 'They're all going to say no. I have no collateral. I have very little revenue. They don't know what a software company is. I'm in my early twenties; I look like I'm fifteen.' They can't call my dad who's a basketball coach in a small town and say, 'You're part of our set of people.' In the set theory of bankers, I was nowhere."

From Winblad to Tilton, the innovators have adapted to the strategies needed and overcome whatever barriers have arisen to capture the necessary capital. They have shown themselves as fighters, who move past "perfection, procrastination, paralysis," because of their commitment to and belief in their business, their team, and themselves. These women have succeeded and show hope for others, but funding is clearly still a major hurdle for women. As put by Winblad, "if you really have a business that makes sense and especially one that's operating and is making sense, you still are going to run into obstacles. Be extremely creative. Think outside of the box. Otherwise, you're going to end up in the box."

---

[59] "The 2013 State of Women-Owned Businesses Report," American Express OPEN, 2013.

[60] "2013CF-The Crowdfunding Industry Report," Massolution, 2013.

[61] Catherine Clifford, "Crowdfunding Industry on Fire: Trends to Watch," *Entrepreneur*, April 8, 2013.

CHAPTER 9
TRANSFORMING THE SYSTEM

When it comes to tech, women are having their say—and they're doing it at the White House. On July 31, 2013, the White House hosted a Champions of Change Tech Inclusion Event. In the morning, forty-two leaders, including six men, gathered in an Eisenhower Executive Office conference room. The conference attendees could choose their morning workshop; so many chose to attend the Girls N' Tech session that it was standing room only. Attendees ranged from high schoolers with Girls Inc.; to nonprofit organizers; to Ruthe Farmer, the director of strategic initiatives of the National Center for Women & Information Technology. Going around the room, each shared their concerns about the lack of girls entering the fields of STEM and how this prompted them to focus on changing this trend. Along the pipeline, they discussed how girls drop out of the field.

Kirsi Kuutti shared how up until age thirteen she wanted to be a ballerina, but then realized this was not the path for her. Lost in high school without ballet, she joined a team to compete in the FIRST (For Inspiration and Recognition of Science and Technology) Robotics competition, an international high school tournament. The first project they built was a soccer-playing robot. At the beginning of the season, one of her friends asked her about her future career goals, saying, "You're going to stick to marketing, right? You're not really going to do any other tech stuff?" In response, she told them she was going to be the captain of the team in the future. Today, Kuutti is a student at University of Minnesota Duluth, studying computer science and electrical engineering and just finished a summer internship at NASA. Her story illustrates the attitudes discouraging girls from entering the field and how events like this one at the White House bring together people determined to open up STEM opportunities for women.

We've discussed how companies, organizations, and governments have worked to embrace and benefit from their female employees. We also want to recognize the individual actions innovative women have taken in order to be more effective in their personal and professional lives; in other words, explore lessons women can use in the workplace.

Quendrith Johnson explained, "We are in the middle of a revolution in working and living. What stems (pun intended) from this is a need for a ground zero rethink on corporate structures and gender dynamics as they relate to child-rearing and literally every aspect of working."

How, as individuals, these innovating women reached personal and professional fulfillment required the mastery of communication techniques, the mindset of an entrepreneur, and the collective power of women working together.

Just as huge shoulder pads and boxy women's suits went out of fashion, so are hyper-masculine communication styles falling out of favor. In fall 2012, John Gerzema and Michael D'Antonio, authors of *The Athena Doctrine: How Women (And the Men Who Think Like Them) Will Rule the Future*, set out to identify what traits make a successful, modern leader. The team interviewed 64,000 people in thirteen countries that, combined, represent about two-thirds of the world's GDP. They asked half the sample to gender-qualify 125 traits. The other half was asked to rank the non-gender-labeled leadership traits in relation to importance in being a successful leader. Their results found that most of the traits correlated with being a good leader, such as "plans for future," "expressive," and "reasonable," were marked as more feminine competencies. Furthermore, 66 percent of those surveyed agreed that the world would be a better place if men thought more like women.[62]

---

[62] John Gerzema and Michael D'Antonio, "The Athena Doctrine: How Women (and the Men Who Think Like Them) Will Rule the Future,"

Gerzema explained his goals for his research: "What I'm trying to do is advocate for women and girls by revealing this portrait of this modern leader and really claiming these traits and values—not as belonging to one gender—and really understanding that we all have these skills, these traits, these ideas, and we can leverage them for competitive advantage." He added, "I would really urge women to understand that the way they think and the values that they have are incredibly important today to driving innovation in the future."

According to a Watson Wyatt study, companies that are highly effective communicators had 47 percent higher total returns to shareholders over five years relative to least effective communicator firms.[63] Clearly harnessing the strength of communication is valuable to proving your value within an organization and to effectively create change. The research by Gerzema and his coauthor showed a growing and global regard for leadership traits associated with women. And many of the people we interviewed for *Innovating Women* assert that there are gender differences in the way people communicate, too.

However, communication styles need to be adapted to the specific work environment. Nikki Barua said, "So many young women come to me seeking mentoring—but they approach me almost apologetically, as if they are sorry about wasting my time. Young men come up to me and pitch me about how driven they are and how mentoring them would be of value to me. Women are much more tentative and cautious while men are far more self-assured and aggressive." Barua added, "I lead with a distinctly feminine style—coach not boss, openly expressing my vulnerability and empathy, rallying people and tapping into my intuition to go beyond just the data. It's been a process growing into my own skin and letting my natural style emerge regardless of whether it was considered acceptable." However, she also mentions how different professional environments require

(San Francisco: Jossey-Bass, 2013).

[63] "Capitalizing on Effective Communication: How Courage, Innovation and Discipline Drive Business Results in Challenging Times," Watson Wyatt Worldwide, 2009/2010.

different styles of communication. For example, traditional and formal work environments often require a more masculine approach. Even so, being tough did not mean entirely sacrificing her feminine leadership style.

One key point that came up in our discussion boards was not to be afraid of sexist slurs, including the "B" word. An 1811 dictionary defines "bitch" as "the most offensive appellation that can be given to an English woman," but it was not until the Gatsby Era that the word was used prominently to criticize women.[64] There are definitely women who undermine others, burn bridges, and sacrifice relationships, but other women use "bitch" as a private rallying cry to prepare them for tough situations and decisions. "If I need to switch it up a little or if I know I have to go into battle that day," explained Sovita Chander, the cofounder and VP of marketing at Caristix, "here's what I do to prep. On the way to work, I tell myself, 'I am one tough bitch.' I OWN that word. And I play the Immigrant Song by Led Zeppelin loudly. That sets me up to get centered and tougher emotionally when I need to be."

Being called a bitch doesn't mean you are one. Today, it is still used against many women in power. Hillary Clinton, Oprah Winfrey, Martha Stewart, Marissa Mayer, Sheryl Sandberg, and Michelle Obama have all been called this name. This proves 'role model' and women who have been called 'bitch' are not mutually exclusive groups, showing how often the word is used to undermine powerful women.

As described by Allannah Rodrigues-Smith, founder and managing director of Europe at Get P3M: "Social conditioning also means that women who behave differently to the expected norms (e.g. 'alpha females') are criticized and labeled in ways that are very different to men—so a dominant man might be described as a 'strong leader' while a dominant female may be branded 'difficult,' 'bossy,' or simply 'a bitch.'"

Landing on the other side of the spectrum, being too

---

[64] Zoë Triska, "You Say 'Bitch' Like It's A Bad Thing: Examining the Implications of the Notorious Word," *The Huffington Post,* January 23, 2013.

passive can hold women back. Looking at the descriptors used in recommendation letters, a recent Rice University study found that being 'too nice' can be detrimental to women's careers: "Female candidates were described in more communal (social or emotive) terms and male candidates in more agentic (active or assertive) terms." With personal information and pronouns scrubbed away, the strength of the recommendation letters were rated. The study found that the more communal the focus, the lower the letters ranked in likelihood of a candidate to be hired.[65]

Ellen Pearlman, president at Pearlman Consulting, shares how she dealt with finding a balance between passive and aggressive in her career: "Early on in my career, when I was starting to get some recognition and promotions, a no-nonsense, hard-headed boss looked at me sternly and asked, 'Do you think you're too nice?' I can't remember now what this was in reference to, but I do recall I had the presence of mind to utter: 'There's more than one way to get results.' I certainly didn't convince him I was right. And I barely convinced myself. Over the years, my niceness became more of a plus. It became empathy. As a manager, I could always put myself in someone else's shoes and see their side. Often that was a good thing and gave me the ability to understand people and their motivations. Most employees blossomed with this style of management. And I began to feel more confident about blending my nice side with my strong side." She found a balance in which she could empower her employees, but maintain respect and authority.

Our ambassadors also provided advice on how to incorporate innovation and an entrepreneurial mindset into performing at the office and thinking about their careers. A lot of this focused on how to view competition, set goals, trust in one's self and instinct, and forever be a student. Many mentioned that the traditional image of masculine competition pits one person or team against another. They suggested that

---

[65] Michelle R. Hebl, Juan M. Madera, and Randi C. Martin. "Gender and Letters of Recommendation for Academia: Agentic and Communal Differences." *Journal of Applied Psychology.* 2009, Vol. 94, No. 6, 1591-1599.

individuals should focus on competing against themselves to create new milestones and reach new heights in their own lives. Yes, two people within an organization may be gunning for the same job, but in the end, their career goals are to achieve what best fits theirs skills and their abilities. "In STEM in particular, emotions are considered bad. 'Don't get emotionally attached to your work.' I consider that the male influence. The only emotion male managers deploy is competition. Female managers harness a wider range of emotions," said Ana Redmond, CEO and software developer at Infinut.com. Adding value is about the bigger picture.

Quotas

DANIELLA ALPHER

Daniella Alpher blogs and tweets about career women globally from her home in Tel Aviv. In her day job, she is a VP of marketing at CoolaData, an open data infrastructure enabling deep behavioral analytics to visualize, predict, and act on data. Daniella spent eight years as a television news producer at ABC News in New York and was awarded an Emmy for millennium coverage and a Peabody for news of the September 11 terrorist attacks.

Dr. Silvija Seres is an independent board member based in Oslo, Norway. She serves as a nonexecutive director of Norwegian Lottery, Aschehoug, and Enoro AS. She has also been a member of the Corporate Assembly at Telenor ASA since 2011 and a member of Telenor's Election Committee since 2012. Previously, Silvija worked as director of business management at Microsoft and as vice president of product marketing at Fast Search & Transfer ASA. Dr. Seres holds a PhD in mathematical sciences from Oxford University and an MBA from INSEAD.

Originally from Serbia and Hungary, Silvija Seres lives in Norway and serves on a dozen company boards ranging from large multinational corporations to small nonprofits. Before her career in technology and business, she worked as an academic, researcher, and programmer in the UK, Saudi Arabia, and Silicon Valley. In 2004, after getting her MBA, Silvija moved back to Oslo with her husband and joined FAST, an enterprise search software company which was acquired by Microsoft four years later.

Silvija has clearly benefitted from being in one of the most gender-equal countries in the world. Parental leave in Norway is almost a full year, and its terms are the most progressive in the world: the first nine weeks can only be taken by mothers, but beyond that, partners can share the leave and fathers are obliged to take at least twelve weeks of leave. Silvija has four small children. "My husband takes almost as long a parental leave as I do," she explained. "Of course it has an effect on his career, but children are not just a woman's issue."

In 2003, Norway was the first country to legislate a 40 percent quota for women on executive boards. At the time, only 7 percent of board directors were women and now the numbers speak for themselves: in 2006, women made up 21 percent of boards, and today they hold nearly half of Norway's corporate board positions.

Typically Norwegian board members used to be recruited from CEO positions in the same or similar industries. Since there were not enough female candidates in those positions, today's Norwegian female board members have less top-level management experience, but more education and deeper industry expertise. Many of these women are also younger than their male colleagues. "This diversity in background leads to more creativity, I think," said Silvija. "The new dynamics in many board rooms have been surprisingly positive."

Silvija had a boss who once asked her why she feels like she has to deliver 150 percent all the time. "I was so focused on proving results and playing by the rules," she admitted. "I over delivered, and some of it was wasted. What I've learned is you should spend only 80 percent of your working time doing real work because if you're efficient, you'll still deliver more than what's expected. Then spend the remaining 20 percent of your time on relationships and talking to people. Women should relax a little bit. It doesn't mean you're not a top boss or anything; it just means that you're a little bit more aware of interpersonal dynamics. Leave some energy for that."

A few years ago, Silvija's boss invited her team to the

United States for a conference, and he dedicated one day to team-building on a golf course. "I said, 'Well, I don't play golf,'" she recalls, "but everybody else was so keen that we went playing golf, and basically what happened is that, you know, they dumped me on this beautiful course and just left. And I said, 'Maybe I should at least be sitting in a cart following you guys or something,' but there wasn't space, or whatever, I don't remember. And so I was kind of left there, six or seven months pregnant, while they were off playing golf for hours."

Silvija had a talk with her boss about it later, and he acknowledged that it wasn't the most sensitive thing to do. She then moved on without missing a beat. There is no chip on her shoulder; it isn't worth her time to stop and dwell because there's just too much going on out there. She clearly had the right skills at the right time when quotas were legislated in Norway. She sits on the boards of the Norwegian Lottery and Statkraft, one of the largest global companies dealing with renewable energy. But while we're likely to see more and more opportunities for women on company boards across the globe, Silvija said it remains a highly competitive environment.

"When quotas were introduced in Norway," she explained, "a lot of women expected these board positions would rain on them. They don't if you're not good at presenting your value. There is no easy, quick way to get on a board. You can't be sure you'll get it even if you do everything right. I've been extremely lucky to get these, even in Norway. We have quotas, but I grounded myself as a technology specialist who knows how to be commercial. It's a matter of being specifically relevant while actively collaborating with the right people. It's a time-consuming exercise—my calendar for the next year is already fully set."

Women hold only 4 percent of the top management positions of public companies in Norway, which means that management suites of Norwegian companies are still heavily dominated by men. Norwegian corporate boards are gender-balanced, but women's pipeline to the top still has a long way to go.

The Big Picture

If a woman focuses on competing with herself, she can set goals that fit the bigger picture of her career. "The most useful lessons/advice I've learned about how to succeed was the fact that I was constantly told that I always could do better. This has encouraged me to compete with myself and to set the bar higher for each of my attempts," explained Angela Lee Foreman, the cofounder, CEO, and chairperson of Thriving Table, Inc. "Another useful piece of advice was that I needed to constantly allow myself to get outside of my comfort zone, which had allowed me to grow and enrich myself as a human being." As Foreman explained, being in your comfort zone does not lead to dramatic growth. It is the challenges and failures that create concrete understanding. Knowing what not to do is often the first step in knowing what will lead to the correct path.

Feeling comfortable outside your comfort zone coupled with thinking outside the box is one true sign of an innovator. In a work setting, this involves thinking past what is *provided* to what is actually *needed*. "It's easier to ask forgiveness than ask for permission," said Pearlman. "That piece of advice can be helpful if you've been raised to stick to the rules. I learned in business (from men) that breaking rules can be very useful. If you succeed, then bosses care less about how you got there." That can mean taking a risk on a project or even requesting necessary training. As Maya Mathias, author of *How To Innovate: Volume 1: Unleash Your InnoMojo* and founder at Inventive Links, recommends, "Don't count on the organization to read your mind and give you the training and development you need. If you feel ill-equipped skill-wise, speak up and ask for what you need. That advice has served me well. Bosses would rather you admit to what you don't know than to fake it and potentially create a bigger mess down the road."

Women need to not only look outside the immediate opportunities they have at work, but when viewing their career, not just look at the position above them, but the bigger picture of what they want to achieve. Innovators do not confine themselves to one career track, but instead look at where they can grow and follow their passion. As Sheryl Sandberg puts it in *Lean In*, attributing the metaphor to *Fortune* magazine editor Pattie Sellers, her career climb wasn't up a ladder: "A jungle gym scramble is the best description of my career."

But the jungle gym scramble is not linear, and sometimes it's hard to decide when to leap. Bhramara Tirupati, innovation instigator and community builder at The Inovo Institute, cautioned women against taking misguided career advice: "People, even well-meaning mentors, often put us in a box based on their own experiences or understanding of how things work. The truth is you won't know what you are capable of unless you try it." Jennifer Argüello, senior tech advisor for the Kapor Center for Social Impact, explained how she often jumped around in her career to learn new skills. All she learned came together to prepare her for her current position. "My career has not been linear. Looking back, I can see a narrative that explains where I am now. I was looking for work every two years early on in my career because the startups I worked for would die. This gave me tremendous resiliency to pick myself up and find new work. I've always kept an arc of a max of eighteen months doing the same job. As time has gone by, that arc has tended to shrink as I traverse from one role to the next. I see all the dots, and now it's time to connect them. As an engineer, I learned how to build technically sound systems that were robust and got the job done. As a product manager, I learned how to listen to the consumer and drive teams to build products people love. As a consultant, I learned how to work with large global enterprises and build customized solutions. As a project manager, I know how to get things done on time, under budget, without burning out my team. As a community organizer, I know how to rally and mobilize people for the cause. And lastly, as a teacher, I know how to impart knowledge and show people how to learn. I have a really good mix of skills to reach my goals, and where I am lacking, I have the capacity to learn what I need to learn to get to the next step." Instead of waiting for a promotion, she trusted her instinct and moved from a position when she felt she was no longer exponentially learning or being challenged. This compass directed her path.

Danae Ringelmann, the founder of Indiegogo, had no idea she would move from Wall Street to developing a crowdfunding platform. Ringelmann accredits the site to following everyday cues, "connecting the dots as they appeared in front of me, and being true to that. I had to start a company to solve a problem that I was feeling, facing, and witnessing every single day"— the problem of inefficient access to capital for innovators and creators. After Indiegogo launched, other crowdfunding platforms emerged, including Kickstarter. Ringelmann added, "All I was doing was paying attention to where my heart was leading my questioning mind every day, and that lead to me starting Indiegogo."

Following gut intuition was a common theme among our ambassadors. A study at Canada's University of Alberta found that the unconscious can sometimes play a role in helping us achieve a long-term or ongoing goal. The study gave some participants flashes of achievement-related words (like "strive" and "succeed") for just microseconds at a time before an unrelated test. The participants didn't consciously realize what they were seeing, but it changed their attitudes, in a subsequent part of the study, toward keywords related to achievement. The study states, "This pattern of findings supports our prediction that with an ongoing goal, such as achievement, that does not have a clear end point or 'finish line,' people continue to strive toward it after success experiences."[66]

This study is supported by the approach of many

---

[66] Sarah G. Moore, Melissa J. Ferguson, and Tanya L. Chartrand. "Affect in the Aftermath: How Goal Pursuit Influences Implicit Evaluations." *Psychology Press.* 2011. P. 453-465.

ambassadors. "I agree that following your instincts is key to success. I rely on them. They are telling me things that I may not yet consciously recognize. I know instinctively if something is wrong with my kids before I can articulate it. Same for business. I know what's the right thing to do before I can articulate it and definitely long before I will see any results that I can show others as proof," explained Ana Redmond, CEO and software developer at Infinut.com. From her own experience, "I don't agree that risk-taking is against following one's instincts. I can take far more risk if I trust my instincts. It's calculated risk in the sense that I rely on the whole picture as I see it, not just a portion of it if I was breaking it down into constituent pros and cons or dollar amounts. But following my instincts makes it harder to explain to others (men or women) why I am making a particular decision. That is something I am still working on."

Libby Leffler, strategic partner manager at Facebook, had an interesting inflection point in her career where she followed her instinct…but with a slight delay. She'd been working at Google as a strategist in Online Sales and Operations, but in 2008, Leffler was recruited to go work for Facebook. "I ended up not accepting the opportunity to move right away," she said. "Google was a huge company. When I was there, there were probably twenty thousand people working there. The idea of leaving all of that to go to the unknown was pretty daunting. I was supposed to join a team of five or six people at Facebook, and it was a small company at the time and really, there was absolutely no way for me to know what it would become." So she kept her job and spent the next few weeks musing about her decision. She believed in the mission of the company, Facebook's desire to create a more connected world. "I mean, there was just a ton of opportunity for me at Facebook. I was really just eager to make an impact and have an almost entrepreneurial experience within a company. So that's what pushed me to end up moving to go work at Facebook in 2008." Since then, she went on to work as Sheryl Sandberg's business lead at Facebook from 2009 to 2012 before moving to run partnerships in 2012.

Besides following intuition, another key skill, according to our ambassadors, is to 'forever be a student.' It is difficult to be creative if one does not absorb like a sponge all the newness and vibrancy of the world around them. "Learning never stops," advises Laura Karolchik, owner/creative director at Mobile Chik. "I have witnessed many in technology unable to continue to work in their field because they won't keep up with changes. Always keep up, attend webinars, seminars, workshops, and take classes. Technology is ever evolving, and you have to keep up to play the game."

Learning and teaching go hand in hand. Mathias explained what enriches her life most: "Two consistently fulfilling threads have emerged through my eclectic work path so far: (1) the opportunity to accumulate new knowledge and master new skills and (2) the chance to nurture talent and human potential in my work teams and for my clients. Personal growth is an ever-constant goal I hold for myself and others—this is the fuel that gets me out of bed each day and raring to go." Women have worked hard to break through barriers within their careers, but to create change, these learnings need to be shared.

When tackling biases, awareness is the first step. Nikki Barua emphasizes this as a major catalyst for change: "Engage in the discussion and drive more awareness. Make the role models visible so other women follow. Openly express your support for change within your organization."

Events and books, including the White House Tech Inclusion day, *Lean In* by Sheryl Sandberg, and *The Athena Doctrine* by John Gerzema and Michael D'Antonio, among others, have been great at opening up discussion about these issues. As more women reach the top, there will be a domino effect in policies and cultures that will help women at all levels.

To transform the fields of STEM and entrepreneurship into a more welcoming place for young women to expand their network and to feel the fulfillment Mathias mentioned, women need to come together and act as role models and mentors to and for each other. As we discussed through the many ambassadors we've spoken to who have created change, many have felt the wake of those before them. Role models need to be tangible.

Women can create change through making themselves available and relatable to those climbing the jungle gym above and below them. Pearlman described the impact of this bottom-up change:

"I hope that as more women move into leadership positions, women in entry or staff positions will be more encouraged to raise their own career aspirations. When women in the executive suite are no longer a rarity, then perhaps female leaders will not feel they need to be just like the men who came before them and will feel free to encourage and reward more feminine strengths in the workplace, such as collaboration, consensus management, and managing through encouragement and not fear. A more supportive work environment would benefit men as well as women."

In the end, women need to support women—and, of course, both genders need to support each other. It is easier to take risks when you know there's a safety net below. Women need to provide each other with that support network, encouragement, and advice that can prepare them to aim high and climb higher. As we've discussed throughout *Innovating Women*, there are numerous hurdles. Our ambassadors have shared ways to overcome obstacles and tactics for tackling day-to-day dilemmas. Even a quick recommendation or compliment after a meeting can have a big impact on another woman's career. Changing the future of innovation requires women to support each other and for all people to reward and respect the virtuous circle of underutilized power in women who innovate.

CHAPTER 10
HOW THE TECH INDUSTRY IS CHANGING —AND HOW WE CAN MAKE IT BETTER

Vivek Wadhwa

In chapter after chapter of this book, you have read inspiring stories of innovating women who defied the odds and achieved success. Each had a different background, motivation, and potential. Each had a different path to success. There was no single problem or solution. That is why we decided to crowdcreate this book—so that we can learn from women from different walks of life, all over the world. Every woman's circumstance is different, and each must look within herself to understand what it will take for her to rise and achieve her potential. To increase the chances of success, they must learn from the experiences of others and work together.

It is no doubt harder for women to gain funding, mentorship, support, and connections than it is for men. The deck has been stacked against them. Women see the technology industry as a boys club, so they are shying away from studying computer science. Their proportion in computer science programs dropped from 37 percent in 1987 to 18 percent by 2012. When women join technology companies, they often get discouraged because they are the only women in a group and are treated differently from everyone else, or they are discriminated against—either deliberately or because of a subconscious bias. When women choose to start technology companies, they face rejection—and abuse—by a venture capital system that is dominated by males. Dan Primack of *Fortune* magazine calculated[67] that as of 2014, only 4 percent of senior investment partners at venture firms are women—and he found none at the heavy-hitters. Heidi Roizen brought to light the perils that women face in her very powerful essay. Few women are able to navigate these treacherous waters.

But things are changing for the better on all of these fronts, especially in Silicon Valley. There is a growing awareness of the problem, solutions are being discussed and implemented, women are beginning to help each other, and the venture capital system is looking at itself critically and mending its ways. Most importantly, as we will discuss in the next chapter, the investment community is becoming less relevant because the cost of creating world-changing technologies is dropping dramatically and allowing women as well as liberated men to work on solving real world problems using exponential technologies.

First, Admit There Is a Problem

With any social problem, the tendency is to first deny it exists and then to blame the victim. Silicon Valley has considered itself to be the perfect meritocracy—it can do no wrong. Admitting that there may indeed be a problem has held its evolution back.

When, in Feb 2010, I wrote the piece for TechCrunch titled "Silicon Valley: You and Some of Your VCs have a Gender Problem," not only did it create a firestorm on social media, but it—and articles by journalists who had views similar to mine—triggered off a series of defensive blogs and commentary. The central argument was that men were very interested in promoting and helping women, but there are too few women in the technology space because it is not for them—that they lacked the capability, motivation, or interest.

These blogs weren't just written by men; some women also chimed in. A few venture capitalists and technology company

---

[67] Dan Primack, "Venture capital's stunning lack of female decision-makers." *Fortune*, February 6, 2014. http://fortune.com/2014/02/06/venture-capitals-stunning-lack-of-female-decision-makers/

executives endorsed and promoted these on social media. There was a barrage of negative comments, such as those I detailed in the introduction.

Women who speak up are used to barrages of angry and sometimes hateful comments. I can only imagine how they must feel. I was really shaken up at having my academic credentials challenged and being called a fraud. I was grateful for the strong support from two of Silicon Valley's most respected entrepreneurs: Eric Ries and Brad Feld, who wrote on his blog:

> *I'm extremely impressed with Vivek Wadhwa's posts on TechCrunch. He's been blogging periodically for them since last fall and has shown that he's willing to take on difficult, controversial, and complicated issues and discuss them in data-driven and systematic ways...The comments, however, were really enlightening to me. The amount of anger and hostility, especially irrational attacks, surprised me. Well—I guess it only surprised me a little—it mostly disappointed me.*[68]

But in May 2014, I was invited to give two talks about women in technology at the National Venture Capital Association's (NVCA) marquee conference, Venturescape. I asked Venky Ganesan, who was chairing the event and had invited me, whether I was walking into some kind of ambush. I joked on Twitter that I felt like a hen going into the foxhouse. After all, the group that I had been most vigorously attacking had offered to put me on center stage and let me speak my mind.

I could not believe the respect I was shown at the event and that the audience of VCs cheered when I criticized their system for being male-dominated and demanded that it be changed. Senior executives of NVCA also told me that they agreed that their member firms needed to be proactive in correcting the gender imbalance. They agreed with what I had asked—that VC firms publish diversity data on their investments and that

---

[68] Brad Feld, "Things Woman Entrepreneurs Can Learn from Indian Entrepreneurs." *FeldThoughts*, February 21st, 2010. http://www.feld. com/wp/archives/2010/02/things-women-entrepreneurs-can-learn-from-indian-entrepreneurs.html

the NVCA should showcase firms that are exemplary. Venture capitalist Jeff Bussgang, who was on a panel with me, also wrote a blog for Huffington Post, "Cultural Dysfunction: The Lack of Women in VC." He acknowledged that there was a system-wide problem, discussed remedies, and concluded, "As with any hard problem, there is no silver bullet. But asking hard questions is what VCs are supposed to be good at, and this is an area where some really hard questions need to be asked."

For all the bad things you can say about Silicon Valley and venture capitalists, you have to give them credit for being open to criticism, listening very carefully, and being proactive in bettering themselves. This is what gives Silicon Valley a global advantage: dissent is encouraged, and learning and reinvention are the norm. There is nothing wrong with saying I made a mistake and am now doing things differently. They even have a special word for failure in the valley: it is called "pivoting."

Today, there is a chorus of female and male bloggers, business executives, and venture capitalists who are openly discussing the problems and solutions. Silicon Valley is pivoting. The prominent investors who were attacking me for writing about gender discrimination have largely gone silent on this issue. Not a peep of disagreement or disparaging word dares to come from them anymore.

IT STARTS FROM THE TOP

The gender imbalance is not only endemic in the lower echelons; it is even worse in the executive ranks and on the boards of technology firms. There are few women in senior executive positions and even fewer on boards. African-Americans and Latinos are practically nonexistent.

The problems start at the top and flow down through the ranks. That is why the boards need to be fixed first.

Twitter made big waves when it revealed its IPO filing in October 2013. This showed that all of Twitter's board members were male, as were all of its executives, other than one lawyer whom the company added a few weeks earlier, and all of its key investors. In an interview with Claire Miller of the *New York Times*, I said that this exemplified the elite arrogance of the Silicon Valley mafia, the Twitter mafia, and its male chauvinistic thinking; how dare they think they could get away with this?

You can't blame a technology startup for having a board that looks like a boys club while it is a private entity because it can't usually pick and choose its investors. They make board seats a condition of their investment. But everything changes when a company goes public. The duty of a board is to look after the interests of all shareholders and to maximize the company's value—not just the few that originally invested in it and reaped fortunes. It isn't about diversity for the sake of diversity. Having women on boards produces better outcomes. Companies with the highest proportions of women board directors outperform those with the lowest proportions by 53 percent. They have a 42 percent higher return on sales and a 66 percent higher return on invested capital. A board that reflects a company's user base is more likely also to understand its market needs and to develop better marketing strategies.

Rather than respond to the issue, Twitter CEO Dick Costolo chose to attack me by tweeting "Vivek Wadhwa is the Carrot Top of academic sources," and several of Silicon Valley's moguls favorited or retweeted his message (this usually implies endorsement or support). But, fortunately, things had progressed enough that there was uproar about his comments. There were hundreds of articles in the press, and men and women both expressed strong disapproval on social media and in blogs.

I didn't for a moment think that Dick Costolo was (or is) sexist or that he deliberately discriminates; he was just reflecting the frat boy behavior that is common in Silicon Valley. This may have been okay when the tech industry was in its infancy and companies such as Twitter didn't get the national attention they do now. But in this day and age, they cannot get away with it.

Twitter handled this matter very badly—despite loud calls to add women to the board, they refused to budge for weeks. This is really bad public relations strategy because it made the criticism get louder. Finally, the company announced the addition of a board member: Marjorie Scardino, former chief executive of publishing giant Pearson. Since then, there has been a flurry of announcements of technology companies adding woman board members. Twitter's PR bungle may have accelerated important progress.

One woman board member isn't enough, however, no matter how competent or outspoken she is. Research shows that board productivity increases the most when there are three or more women on boards. So a lot more needs to be done at Twitter and other companies.

Technology companies have a lot to be embarrassed about when it comes to gender diversity. If they released gender and race diversity data, it would shine a light on their flawed employment practices and the public would apply pressure for change. That is why they have steadfastly refused to release these.

In 2008, Mike Swift, of the *San Jose Mercury News*, began probing the topic of gender and race diversity by sending Freedom of Information Act requests to Silicon Valley's fifteen largest employers. He lost an eighteen-month battle with five of the top companies.

In 2011, CNN launched its investigation and demanded data from twenty of the most influential U.S. technology companies, the Department of Labor, and the Equal Employment Opportunity Commission. It filed two Freedom of Information Act requests for workforce diversity data. Only Dell, Ingram Micro, and Intel complied. Later it forced the Department of Labor to release what data it had for Cisco and Ebay. Apple, Google, Hewlett-Packard, IBM, and Microsoft all successfully petitioned the Department of Labor for their data to be excluded because releasing it would cause "competitive harm." Several companies gave CNN the familiar excuse: that they had a "pipeline problem" because too few women and members of ethnic minorities are graduating with technical degrees.

The data that was available revealed what we would expect: that the numbers of women are extremely low and Hispanics and African-Americans are hardly to be found.

In October 2013, a young engineer at Pinterest —an

innovating woman—Tracy Chou decided to do something about this herself. She set up an open-source spreadsheet on Github to collect gender data. She asked her friends and their friends to input data about the companies or departments that they worked at.

In March 2014, Rev. Jesse Jackson joined the fray by leading a delegation to Hewlett-Packard's annual shareholders to bring attention to Silicon Valley's poor record of including blacks and Latinos in hiring, board appointments, and startup funding.

The breakthrough came on May 25, 2014, when Google broke ranks with the technology industry and released its diversity data. It revealed that only 17 percent of its technology workforce was female—not impressive, but better than most. And Google pledged to work toward increasing that figure.

Google's breaking ranks had the very positive effect that I expected it would. On June 12, 2014, LinkedIn followed suit and released its gender data. Its workforce is 61 percent male and 53 percent white compared to Google, which is 70 percent male and 61 percent white. It did not break the data down by engineering, most likely because it would have fared worse than Google. On June 17, 2014, Yahoo! released it numbers: only 15 percent of its technology workforce is female. It, too, pledged to increase diversity. On June 25, Facebook chimed in with their numbers (15 percent female) and pledge.

I expect that many other companies will follow suit. At the least, they are looking at themselves more closely in the mirror.

How to Correct the Gender Gap

A common excuse for the lack of women in technology companies is that women simply aren't available. I heard the same from a startup, Humin, that I have been mentoring and joined the board of.

"We'd love to have women on our engineering team, but we just can't find any—no matter how hard we try. I know that we need to have a team that understands the product needs of more than just the young male user," said founder Ankur Jain

Humin's first board meeting in May 2013.

"Not good enough; change the recruiting specs, network with women's groups, do whatever it takes," was my response. I was being uncharacteristically harsh to a young man I considered to be extremely brilliant and open-minded. I knew I wasn't being reasonable, but considered it my responsibility as a board member to raise this important issue. Ankur and his three college buddies had just moved their mobile-software-platform startup to San Francisco. Competition for talent is fierce in Silicon Valley, and it is difficult for startups to compete with the likes of Google and Facebook—which sometimes offer million-dollar sign-up packages.

I advised the Humin team to network with women's groups and look harder. And that is what they did. Humin's VP of product and engineering, Percy Rajani, revamped their interviewing process to look for top talent in unconventional places rather than just looking for former employees of other well-known tech companies. He knew that the company could teach programming languages and processes, but intelligence, motivation, and personality were the key traits to recruit.

Humin did succeed in assembling an exceptional and diverse engineering team. By broadening their search process, they found a depth and breadth of female talent, especially among developers whose original background was in engineering fields outside of computer science. Today, six of Humin's engineering team of 18—or 33 percent—are women. Two of the women are PhDs.

Xerox CTO Sophie Vandebroek also found a way to fix the gender balance in her team by doing in-college hiring and creating a culture and work environment that was appealing to women engineers. More than 40 percent of her teams' engineering departments hire women; in some years, it's more than 50 percent. She takes pride in being able to attract people from all different colors, from different genders, and of different ages.

Technology companies also need to look at who does the hiring and how. "If someone came in right now and announced that the zombie apocalypse had just started outside, what would you do in the next hour? What is something that you're geeky about? What is a superpower you would give to your best friend?" These are the types of questions that many technology companies, including Google, Amazon, Dell, and Dropbox, used to ask interviewees. Interviewers—who tend to be young men—often believe that such questions help them identify creative people, while making the interviews more fun. The problem is that such questions are fun only for people who understand the jokes—and who can think like the interviewers do.

They don't lead to better hiring outcomes, as Google learned. Its senior vice president for people operations, Laszlo Bock, said in a June 2013 interview with the *New York Times*, "…we found that brainteasers are a complete waste of time. How many golf balls can you fit into an airplane? How many gas stations in Manhattan? A complete waste of time. They don't predict anything. They serve primarily to make the interviewer feel smart."

After hearing from concerned female employees at Dropbox about hiring practices there and attempting to contact the CEO and the media relations team, I wrote an article titled "Dropbox's hiring practices explain its disappointing lack of female employees,"[69] criticizing the company in February of 2014.

I quoted Level Playing Field founder Freada Kapor Klein, who said, "Dropbox executives, like other startup founders, honestly believe they are a meritocracy and are unaware as to how hidden bias operates. Employee referrals play a large role in their hiring, as in most startups, which further introduces bias and makes the culture exclusionary…Founders are looking for 'objective' measures, such as school ranking, GPAs, SAT scores, but fail to recognize that these are biased. Dropbox and other startups should pioneer new ways to identify people who

---

[69] Vivek Wadhwa, "Dropbox's hiring practices explain its disappointing lack of female employees." *The Washington Post*, February 14, 2014. http://www.washingtonpost.com/blogs/innovations/wp/2014/02/14/dropboxs-hiring-practices-explain-its-disappointing-lack-of-female-employees/

can succeed on the core set of job responsibilities. Perhaps a question on how Dropbox might be used to solve income inequality or the unaffordability of housing in San Francisco would reveal as much about someone's creativity—and more about their character—than questions about superheroes."

I sent this article to Drew Houston and again asked for a meeting. Drew and his diversity team came to meet me and my colleague Daniel Siciliano at Stanford Law School on March 5, 2014. Drew seemed to be genuinely concerned about the issues I had raised and briefed me on actions that his management team were taking to remedy the hiring situation and fix their gender imbalance. I have since heard from Dropbox employees that it is making good progress on this front.

Dropbox is proving that fixing the gender imbalance really isn't hard once CEOs accept the situation and put a focus on it. Here are some things that companies—big and small—need to do:

1. Look at how jobs are defined. Lucy Sanders, CEO of The National Center for Women & Information Technology, says that companies need to pay attention to what types of technical jobs are given to women. Are they the low-status technical jobs? Are they high-prestige jobs, such as architect and lead designer? How are the jobs defined? Are they written in a way that will solicit a response from males? For example, job descriptions that are overloaded with long lists of required skills (which may or may not be needed on day one and could be learned on the job) may cause women to not apply if they don't have each and every skill; men, on the other hand, will tend to apply if they have only a subset of the skills.

2. Broaden the talent pool by looking beyond the usual recruitment grounds. Companies need to build ties to universities where there are high proportions of women and minorities and to recruit at conferences such as the Grace Hopper Celebration of Women in

Computing and Women 2.0.

3. Interview at least one woman and one member of a minority for every open position. Freada Kapor Klein says companies should implement a rule such as the Rooney Rule for National Football League teams. This requires all teams to interview minority candidates for head coaching and senior football operation jobs. The key is to make sure that every hiring pool is diverse with respect to gender and race. "If women aren't in the candidate pool, they're not going to get hired," says Klein.

4. Have at least one woman on the hiring team. Telle Whitney, CEO of the Anita Borg Institute, cites academic research that shows that people tend to hire those who are similar to them. She says that the demographics of the hiring team greatly influence the outcome of hiring. It also makes a difference in offer acceptance. A female candidate will recognize that the business values diversity if the interviewers are men and women. Whitney says women on the hiring team should be part of the R&D department and in influential positions because having women in senior-level technical roles positively influences the hiring of further technical women.

5. In hiring decisions, the focus should always be on competencies rather than on credentials. Klein says that degrees from prestigious schools usually heavily outweigh any ability to write code or solve problems. Candidate-screening criteria, such as unpaid internships, summer international experiences, and gap years, also create an unfair advantage because these are signs of a wealthy background and not earned meritocratic achievements. She says that companies should focus on "distance traveled"—such as the demonstrated ability of people who grew up in modest circumstances to overcome adversity or being the first in their family to go to college.

Once Women Are Hired, the Challenge for Businesses Becomes How to Retain Them

A problem women commonly face when they join the industry is that of feeling marginalized and discriminated against. They leave the workforce midcareer. A report by the Anita Borg Institute noted that women leave technology companies at twice the rate at which men do. The key reasons are poor working conditions for women, lack of work-life balance, uninteresting work, and bad organizational climate.

Here is what needs to be done:

1. Train managers and hold them responsible. As the Anita Borg Institute report notes, for women in technical roles, managerial support is especially important, as women often experience unconscious bias and additional barriers to advancement. Since managers have such a strong influence on the retention of women in technical roles, it is essential that management training and development incorporate tools to actively encourage collaboration, inclusiveness, and diversity. Achievement of retention goals should be part of a manager's performance evaluation, and managers should be given incentives to take an interest in the professional development of the women technologists reporting to them.

2. Foster an open and collaborative corporate culture. Whitney says women often suffer negative consequences when they express a new or different view. She says that by developing a culture that encourages diverse ideas and perspectives, companies will not only improve job satisfaction for women in technical roles, but also benefit from fresh ideas and approaches to solving important problems.

3. Institute flexible work policies. Companies need to provide both women and men with the ability to take time off for parenting and family, to work from home,

and to have flexible work schedules. Parents should not have to apologize or feel guilty if a child is sick and they need to rush to school.

4. Create effective complaint channels. For issues of harassment and discrimination, there needs to be not just formal mechanisms that require investigations, but informal ombudsmen, mentors, and trusted individuals who can offer practical problem-solving advice. According to Klein, these need to be side by side with formal mechanisms that document how investigations are conducted and resolutions achieved. It is also important to designate who is responsible for handling complaints. Says Klein, "think about how a new young woman employee gets guidance about what to say or do when someone makes a sexist comment and think about someone who wants to raise an allegation of unequal compensation between men and women managers in the company. You'd never want to take both of these situations to the same person and have them handled the same way."

5. Institute sensing, monitoring, and feedback mechanisms. Klein says that companies need to frequently run customized and anonymous surveys on quality of work life, send periodic pulse surveys on topics, conduct exit interviews, and maintain anonymous feedback channels. Well-designed surveys are early warning signals, and good data mining lets the company identify systemic biases, she says. In addition, practices need to be systematically monitored. Assignments, promotions, and performance evaluations all need to be monitored for outcomes. Is there subtle bias in the process? Who are the decision-makers?

All of this needs to come from the top down. Corporate executives must take ownership for increasing technical women's participation. If they don't, it won't happen. Managers must review data at every level of the pipeline with executive management. What you measure, you can control. Most importantly, as Sanders says, "this can't be lip service and can't be delegated to mid-management—and certainly not to the technical women themselves to solve. Make it clear why it's not just a quota issue or an arbitrary mandate, but a critical innovation and business imperative."

One more key point, one that Klein always asks me to stress: It is important to recognize the changing demographics in the United States. The current majority of school kids in many states comprise members of racial and ethnic minorities. Too often, a focus on 'women' has meant affluent, white women. We need to make sure that company culture and practices are welcoming to African-American women, Latinas, and Asian-American women. They are an important part of the future of innovation and of this country.

FOSTERING ENTREPRENEURSHIP

To create the next Google, Facebook, and Intel, we need to boost entrepreneurship—particularly among women. It starts with making cultural changes to make risk-taking—and failure—more acceptable, teaching aspiring entrepreneurs the basics, providing them with seed funding and encouragement, and mentoring them to success. Networks play a very important role, as I know from personal experience as well as from my academic research.

FOLLOWING THE INDIAN TRAIL

Thirty years ago, there were hardly any Silicon Valley firms with Indian-born founders. UC-Berkeley's AnnaLee Saxenian documented that 7 percent of tech companies started in 1980 to 1998 had an Indian founder. A survey conducted by my research team at Duke University found that this proportion had increased to 13.4 percent from 1995 to 2005 and then to 15.5 percent in 2012. These are pretty astonishing numbers considering that according to the U.S. census, in 2000, less than 0.7 percent of the U.S. population and only 6 percent of the Silicon Valley high-tech workforce was born in India.

Indian immigrants didn't have it easy. They suffered from the same types of stereotypes as women, African-Americans, and Hispanics. Despite having cofounded a software company that we took from startup to $120 million in revenue, profitability, and IPO in a record five years, I couldn't get Research Triangle Park (RTP) VCs to even return my phone calls when I was ready to start my second venture. I later found out why: "my people" were great at mathematics and made great engineers, but didn't make great CEOs—"we" didn't have the necessary management skills, didn't like diluting our equity ownership by raising venture capital, and couldn't "fit" into the rough-and-tough American business-management culture. That's what one RTP VC told me over lunch, to explain why his firm wasn't inviting me to pitch my business plan. They were very busy and had to be selective in who they met. Sounds familiar, doesn't it? My "people" didn't fit the pattern that VCs knew would lead to success.

So how did "my people" rise above ignorance and bigotry? When the first generation of Indians in Silicon Valley succeeded in shattering the glass ceiling, they decided to help others follow their path. They realized that they had all surmounted the same obstacles. And they could reduce the barriers to entry for others behind them by sharing their experiences and opening some doors.

In 1992, a number of highly successful Indian business executives formed a group called The Indus Entrepreneurs (which is now called TiE). Their mission was to give back to the community by fostering entrepreneurship. They would hold monthly events, teach entrepreneurship, and provide mentoring and support. And they would facilitate Indian-style matchmaking between entrepreneurs themselves and with investors and corporate partners. They created two categories of members: a charter member, who took the role of Guru, and a regular member, who would be a disciple. The Guru had to donate time and money (minimum $1,500 per year) and was not allowed to gain any personal financial benefit. When disciples achieved success, they would be expected to pass it forward by becoming charter members and helping others behind them.

I was able to get advice and mentoring from a Who's Who of Silicon Valley's TiE group and build a successful business. It wasn't long before the VCs were tripping over each other to offer me term sheets. But while male Indian entrepreneurs today are perceived to fit the patterns of success that VCs look for, women are still left out. (Though TiE set a goal of helping all communities, women are still underrepresented in its ranks.)

Women need to help one another, to have corporate leaders be personally involved in mentoring, proselytizing, and demonstrating by example a different model of investing in women and minority-group entrepreneurs. There is nothing more powerful within an organization than having its own CTO talk about the importance of, for example, promoting women. And we need to have VCs mentor the women and minorities they typically ignore. They need to do this not only for social good, but also for their own survival.

CHAPTER 11
LOOKING TO THE FUTURE

VIVEK WADHWA

The world has many problems to solve. Billions live without reliable energy and lack adequate access to water, health care, and education. More people die from lack of clean water than war. Our food system, which is the primary source of income for billions, must grow to meet the needs of another two billion people. Poverty is endemic on the planet. These are some of humanity's grand challenges—and they're not just in the developing world. Many parts of the developed world also suffer from these ills, particularly in health care, education, and poverty.

The good news is that solutions to these grand challenges are at hand. Several technologies are now advancing exponentially. They enable entrepreneurs to do what only governments and large research labs could do before in solving big problems. Yet Silicon Valley, which could be taking the lead in ridding humanity of its ills, is focused on scoring big hits by solving small problems. The venture capital system, which fuels the technology industry's growth, is geared toward rolling the dice in the hope of receiving returns of five to ten times the invested capital within five to seven years. Such home runs are rare, so the system is in decline. For the last fifteen years, most venture capital firms have produced lower returns than the stock markets.

For these investors, the quickest hits usually come from building apps or games that go viral or websites that automate business processes. Writing software isn't hard—even those who not have completed their college education can do this. They, too, think small and dream of big financial returns. That is why the emphasis is on youth, and Silicon Valley moguls pay teens to drop out of college.

This creates a big opportunity for women who want to solve big problems. Women are beginning to dominate many fields in education and gain an increasing share of the degrees. They now earn 61.6 percent of all associate's degrees, 56.7 percent of all bachelor's degrees, and 58.5 percent of graduate degrees in the United States. More women than men graduate in fields such as biology, education, health sciences, social/behavioral studies, and arts and humanities. In the OECD countries, women constitute 58 percent of all graduates, and more girls than boys now complete their secondary education in thirty-two of thirty-four of these countries. And, of course, girls match boys in mathematical achievement.

In building an exponential technology, education is important, and knowledge of more than one discipline provides a big advantage. And if you combine a cross-disciplinary education with empathy and a desire to do good, you have a powerful combination. That's why many female entrepreneurs are best positioned to solve humanity's grand challenges—and to save the world. And that is why it is important to teach and inspire them.

Not only is the power and capability of certain technologies increasing at an exponential pace, their footprint and costs are declining dramatically. This puts women in the catbird seat. The strong disadvantage they had in not being able to gain venture capital is no longer an inhibitor. World-changing technologies can be built for relatively small amounts of money. Prudent financial management can allow an entrepreneur to bootstrap a startup to the point from which it can gain funding on its own merits.

Let me illustrate some of these technologies. Most people are aware of the advances in computing. They have seen the processing power double every eighteen months—as prices dropped and devices became smaller. A $500 laptop has more computing power today than a Cray 2 supercomputer that cost $17.5 million in 1985. What once required a large building and a water-cooling system now fits in a pocket. In the technology industry, this progression is known as Moore's Law.

Such advances are happening not only in computing, but also in the fields of medicine, robotics, artificial intelligence, synthetic biology, 3-D printing, and medicine. Futurist Ray Kurzweil noted that as any technology becomes an information technology, it starts advancing exponentially. That is what is happening in these fields.

It wasn't long ago when our only recourse when we doubted our doctor's prescription was to seek a second opinion. Now, when we need information about an ailment, we search on the Internet. We have access to more medical knowledge than our doctors used to have via their medical books and journals, and our information is more up-to-date than those medical books were. We can read about the latest medical advances anywhere in the world. We can visit online forums to learn from others with the same symptoms, provide each other with support, and discuss the side effects of our medicines. We can download apps that help us manage our health. All of this can be done by anyone with a smartphone.

Our smartphones also contain a wide array of sensors, including an accelerometer that keeps track of our movement, a high-definition camera that can photograph external ailments and transmit them for analysis, and a global positioning system that knows where we have been. Wearable devices such as Fitbit, Nike, and Jawbone are commonly being used to monitor the intensity of our activity; a heart monitor such as one from Alivecor can display our electrocardiogram; several products on the market can monitor our blood pressure, blood glucose, blood oxygen, respiration, and even our sleep. Soon we will have sensors that analyze our bowel and bladder habits and food intake. All of these will feed data into our smartphones and cloud-based personal lockers. Our smartphone will become a medical device akin to the Star Trek tricorder.

We learned how to sequence the genome about a decade ago, and sequencing it cost billions. Today, a full human genome sequence costs as little as $1,000. At the rate at which prices are dropping, it will cost less within five years than a blood test does today. This makes it affordable to compare one person's DNA with another's, learn what diseases those with similar genetics have had in common, and discover how effective different medications or other interventions were in treating them.

Robots can now perform surgery, milk cows, do military reconnaissance and combat, and fly fighter jets. The robots of today aren't the Androids or Cylons that we used to see in science-fiction movies, but specialized electromechanical devices that are controlled by software and remote controls. As computers become more powerful, so do the abilities of these devices. High school children are using robot-development kits with open-source software to create sophisticated robots. Industrial robots that can do manufacturing and automate other routine processes cost as little as $22,000, and prices are dropping while their capabilities advance to human levels. I expect to be ordering a robot like Rosie from *The Jetsons* sometime in the next decade and to have her delivered to me via an Amazon robotic drone. She will cost less than $22,000 in today's terms.

3-D printers can transform materials such as plastic, ceramics, glass, and titanium into mechanical devices, medical implants, jewelry, and even clothing. The cheapest 3-D printers, which print rudimentary objects, currently sell for between $500 and $1,000. Soon we will have printers for this price that can print toys and household goods. By the end of this decade, we will see 3-D printers doing the small-scale production of previously labor-intensive crafts and goods. In the next decade, we may be 3-D-printing buildings and electronics. Remember the Star Trek replicator? It may not remain science fiction.

Artificial Intelligence (AI) has progressed to the point at which a computer was able to defeat the most capable and knowledgeable humans on the TV show *Jeopardy*. The technology that enabled this, IBM Watson, is now available to developers everywhere. AI systems are being trained to perform medical diagnosis, drive autonomous cars, and operate call centers. They are finding their way into manufacturing and powering robots that do human chores. A Samantha-like companion from the movie *Her* may not be that far away. I expect her—or "Him"— to have a robotic body, though, which is 3-D printed to order. Imagine the possibilities.

Regenerative medicine has been used to implant lab-grown skin, tracheas, and bladders into humans. Soon, 3-D printing technologies will grow human cells, layer by layer, to make replacement skin, body parts, and eventually organs such as hearts, livers, and kidneys. Kinkos-like production shops are also synthesizing DNA, which researchers can use to create new organisms and synthetic life forms. DNA "printing" is priced by the number of base pairs to be assembled (the chemical "bits" that make up a gene). Today's cost is about twenty-eight cents per base pair, and prices are falling dramatically. Within a few years, it could cost a hundredth of this amount. Eventually, like laser printers, DNA printers will be inexpensive home devices. I can't even imagine what we will "print."

Using nanotechnology, engineers and scientists are developing many new types of materials, such as carbon nanotubes, ceramic-matrix nanocomposites (and their metal-matrix and polymer-matrix equivalents), and new carbon fibers. These new materials enable designers to create products that are stronger, lighter, more energy-efficient and more durable than anything that exists today.

And then there is data—lots of it. Over the centuries, we gathered data on things such as climate, demographics, and business and government transactions. Our farmers kept track of the weather so that they would know when to grow their crops, we had land records so that we could own property, and we developed phone books so that we could find people. Now we also gather data on web browsing—what news we read, where we shop, what sites we surf, what music we listen to, what movies we watch, and where we travel. On social media, we gather data about what we like and dislike and who we know and even our sexual preferences and spiritual values. Today, there are more than 100 hours of video uploaded to YouTube every minute, and far more video is being collected worldwide through the surveillance cameras that you see everywhere. Mobile phone apps are keeping track of our every movement—everywhere we go, how fast we move, what time we wake.

Now combine all of this data with the exponential technologies I detailed earlier, and you have the ability to create world changing innovations.

Consider what could happen if we correlated information about a person's genome, lifestyle habits, and locations with their medical history and the medications they take. We would understand the true effectiveness of drugs and their side effects. This would change the way drugs are tested and prescribed. And then, when genome data becomes available for millions, perhaps billions of people, we could discover the correlations between disease and DNA to prescribe personalized medications—tailored to an individual's DNA. We are talking about a revolution in health and medicine.

In schools, classes are usually so large that the teacher does not get to know the student—particularly the child's other classes, habits, and progress through the years. What if a digital tutor could keep track of a child's progress, likes and dislikes, learning preferences, and strengths and weaknesses? Using data gathered by digital learning devices, test scores, attendance, and habits, the teacher could be informed on which students to focus on, what to emphasize, and how best to teach an individual child. This could change the education system itself.

And then combine the data that is available on a person's shopping habits with their social preferences, health, and location. We could have shopping assistants and personal designers creating new products, including clothing that is 3-D printed or custom manufactured for the individual. An IBM Watson-like assistant could anticipate what a person wants to wear or to eat and have it ready for them.

Data can assist human decision-making in almost every sector. Analyzing large amounts of data from different perspectives can unearth new insights and prevent errors. This data can be used to decide where a new store will be located, when to water a field or spray it for insecticides, or when a police car should patrol a neighborhood. It this exponential era, data is the key to competition and productivity.

As I mentioned earlier, all of these advances require more than software coding skills. They require knowledge of fields such as biology, education, health sciences, and human behavior—all of which are fields that women are dominating. Then there is design—which makes technology elegant, usable, and appealing. The key to good design is empathy combined with knowledge of the arts and humanities. Indeed, as Steve Jobs said when he unveiled the iPad 2: "It's in Apple's DNA that technology alone is not enough — it's technology married with liberal arts, married with the humanities that yields us the result that makes our heart sing." Who is better positioned to dominate exponential technology design than women?

The software, hardware, and disk storage needed to start a technology company would have cost millions of dollars a few years ago. Complex computations often required arrays of mini-computers and sometimes supercomputers. Today's laptops have more processing power than these. For storage, you once needed server farms and racks of hard disks; today, you have cloud computing and cloud storage—and they're cheap.

You can also bootstrap hardware companies, such as Nest (which Google acquired for $3.2 billion). Sensors such as those in our smartphones would have cost tens of thousands of dollars a few years ago; they now cost practically nothing. Entrepreneurs on shoestring budgets can build smartphone apps that act as medical assistants to detect disease; body sensors that monitor heart, brain, and body activity; and technologies to detect soil humidity and improve agriculture.

Entrepreneurs once had to begin their journey by writing a detailed business plan and pitching it to venture capitalists. But that is no longer the case because the cost of technology has dropped exponentially. They can beg or borrow the relatively small amounts of money they need from their friends and relatives—or they can crowdfund their startup.

Women no longer have a financing disadvantage that they once had. There is nothing holding them back. They are now excelling in the fields that require more compassion, cross-disciplinary knowledge, and vision. They are building world-changing companies. Some women, such as Anousheh Ansari, are literally shooting for the stars as you will read in her essay ahead.

In an email exchange, one of our ambassadors, Phaedra Pardue, wrote some words that really inspired me. She explained better than I can why it is important to inspire women innovators. Here is what she said:

"I am of Klamath Native American decent. My mother is full-blood Native American, and my father is European and came from English/French settlers that made it to the Pacific Northwest. My Native American ancestors believed that women hold the sacred power to bring life to this world, so therefore in Native American society, women were revered and respected, as equal to men in many ways. In many of the Native American cultures, it was the women's decision whether or not to go to war as a people. Decisions with tribal council included women elders as well as men. There was no fear of their sacred wisdom and power, so there was no need to keep Native American women in a subservient role. They held property and could marry and divorce by choice in most tribes. In fact, often property was passed down along the female line, from mother to daughter. The ancient wisdom of my people that I always try to share when I meet someone who has "never met a real Indian" is that our people made important tribal decisions based on looking forward into the future seven generations. Only once it was deemed to be positive that far into the future was agreement to proceed granted. I always try to share this concept with people; it seems to be hard for many to grasp, but think what an incredible world we would live in if we all tried to think forward in this way, for the good of the ALL. FOR THE GOOD OF THE ALL."

She is completely right. This is for the good of mankind.

From Pondering on the Mysteries of the Universe to Solving the Problems of Health Using Micromachines

DR. ANITA GOEL

Anita Goel, MD, PhD, is the founder, chairman, and CEO of Nanobiosym and a scientist, physicist-physician, inventor, and global entrepreneur. Dr. Goel was awarded the 2013 X Prize for her contributions to the emerging field of nanobiophysics and her inventions for Gene-RADAR®. She has been named among the "World's Top Science and Technology innovators" by MIT's Technology Review *magazine, "Top 10 Women to Watch in Tech" by* Inc., *and one of the "56 Companies That Are Changing the World" by the* Boston Globe, *among numerous other honors and awards.*

I was born in Worcester, Massachusetts, while my dad was completing his surgical residency. At the age of three, my parents and I moved to the little rural town of Prentiss, Mississippi, where my dad was heavily recruited to be the local town surgeon. A few years earlier, President John F. Kennedy had increased the quota of visas for foreign-trained medical graduates to help fill the desperate need for more qualified doctors to serve rural America.

My parents had emigrated from India to pursue the American Dream. We landed in the Deep South of the early 1970s, where black and white people still lived on different sides of the railroad tracks. On my first day of prekindergarten (without any effort on my part), I made local history for the little town of Prentiss by becoming the first nonwhite child to attend its all-white, racially segregated school and Southern Baptist Church. At that young age, I learned not only how easy it was to make history, but also how to survive and thrive at the nexus of many different worlds and silos that did not talk to each other.

In Mississippi, I recall spending a lot of time outdoors meditating in nature, studying the likes of Einstein, Tesla, and Swami Vivekananda, and wondering about the deep mysteries of the universe. I found myself on both an inner and outer quest to discover truth and meaning in the universe, breaking down the silos between my natural curiosity-driven scientific quest to understand the world around me, and my deep inner spiritual yearnings and meditations to know Truth and realize the Self.

I loved physics and mathematics, for they provided me a window through which I could realize a deeper understanding of, and appreciation for, nature. On the other hand, I was exposed to the practical real-world problems of biology and medicine. I would often accompany my dad into his operation theaters and on his rounds at the hospital. By age eight, I was an MD in my own mind. I became convinced that there must be an underlying unity in nature and that the same physics that we use to understand the far reaches of the universe must be applicable to understanding life and living systems and tackling the problems of biomedicine.

However, the deeper I went in my academic pursuits in physics and medicine, first at Stanford for my BS in physics and then at Harvard for an MD and MIT for a PhD in physics, the more aware I became of just how deeply disjointed these seemingly orthogonal fields were in our modern scientific paradigm. Modern physics was developed primarily in the last century in the context of inanimate matter and had not really come to terms with life and consciousness. Modern medicine was currently practiced chiefly at the level of molecular biology and chemistry and had not yet addressed the role that physics plays in fundamental physiological processes.

Once again, I found myself at the nexus of two fascinating worlds that did not talk to each other. In my quest to find an underlying unified framework to bring physics and life on the same footing, I found that the new field of nanotechnology could help me bridge these silos. I was very fortunate along the way to have wonderful mentors, including Nobel Laureates Steve Chu and Dudley Herschbach, who enthusiastically encouraged my curiosity and helped me further this deeper quest by finding practical ways to channel it to advance the frontier of science.

Over the past twenty years, I have been deeply fascinated with the problem of molecular nanomachines that read and write information into DNA and how their real-time dynamics could be studied and controlled using rigorous concepts and experimental tools from physics and nanotechnology. My own theoretical physics work had been focused on extending the framework of modern physics to describe the interplay of matter, energy, and information, but I needed an experimental way to prove my theories. For me, these nanomotors provided a living laboratory to probe the physics of life and experimentally investigate the interplay of matter, energy, and information at the nanoscale. I had been dreaming for years of ways to harness these nanomachines for various breakthrough technological applications.

In 2004, while still in the midst of completing my clinical training at Mass General Hospital and Brigham and Women's as part of the Harvard-MIT and HST MD-PhD Medical Scientist Training Program, I received a chance call from a team of U.S. military and DARPA officers looking to develop next-generation capabilities for pathogen detection for unanticipated threats like anthrax, bioterrorism, and pandemic outbreaks like SARS. They wanted to summon the nation's leading experts across various silos to help tackle these threats to national security. They needed someone who had a "hard-core" physical science background and understood clinical medicine and pathogens and the new field of nanotechnology.

After two hours of intense questioning by an expert panel about my ideas and my relevant expertise, they offered me funding to demonstrate proof of concept of some of my ideas. They also added that they believed I would fail, but wanted to bet on me anyway. When I inquired why they thought I would fail, they explained that the project was very difficult and that they were not giving me enough money or time to achieve the proposed seven milestones; from their perspective, the odds were stacked against me, but because they saw the potential breakthrough nature of the innovation I was proposing, as well as my stellar track record of extraordinary achievements at such a young age, they were willing to take a bet on me despite these odds.

I asked if they were willing to wait until after I completed my six months of clinical work, which was a sixty to eighty hour-a-week work commitment in the hospitals. They said they could not wait and gave me a few minutes to decide whether I wanted to "take it or leave it." Since I was in a military building with no access to call my family, mentors, and advisors for their advice, I decided to meditate and go to that inner space to make my decision.

I said yes to the offer, and six months later, we achieved all seven milestones and two additional ones, resulting in the U.S. government doubling our funding and leading to multiple awards from the U.S. Defense Advanced Research Projects Agency, the U.S. Air Force Office of Scientific Research, the Department of Energy, and the U.S. Defense Threat Reduction Agency. This series of awards helped me to launch the Nanobiosym Research Institute and Incubator in 2004. A few years later, we spun out Nanobiosym Diagnostics to develop and commercialize Gene-RADAR® as a platform for mobilizing, decentralizing, and personalizing the next generation of health care.

I am grateful for visionary organizations like DARPA for investing early on in some of my dreams and providing me with the opportunity to make a quantum leap to manifest those dreams into a reality.

Nearly a decade later, our company Nanobiosym Diagnostics is poised to take the next quantum leap by creating a paradigm shift in global health care that will disrupt the centralized model of the health care industry. Our flagship product, Gene-RADAR®, is a mobile diagnostic platform about the size of an iPad that provides anyone-anytime-anywhere instant access to personalized information about their own health. What Google did for the information industry and what cell phones did for the telecom industry, Nanobiosym is doing for health care. By decentralizing the infrastructure needed to diagnose and manage disease, it will democratize access to health care on a global scale, empowering individuals to take ownership over their own health and providing access to the more than four billion people who currently lack even basic health care.

I strongly believe disruptive technologies alone are not enough to drive the revolution in global health care; we need an entire ecosystem of early adopters and change agents to pilot and integrate these next-gen technologies. Engineering the ecosystem is just as important as the physics and nanotechnology engineering. We stand at a moment in history where innovative technologies and forward-looking thinkers will change the world as we know it by continuing to pursue convergent paths that can work in harmony to provide new opportunities to disrupt our current worldview.

I believe that the next generations of breakthrough innovation and quantum leaps in our science, technology, industries, and humanitarian impact will come at the holistic convergence of traditional silos. The deeper mission of my life and the organizations that I have founded is to infuse a higher level of consciousness in our science, technology, business, and humanitarian impact.

To the Stars

ANOUSHEH ANSARI

Anousheh Ansari is a serial entrepreneur and cofounder and chairman of Prodea Systems, a company that will unleash the power of the Internet to all consumers and dramatically alter and simplify consumers' digital living experience. Prior to founding Prodea Systems, Anousheh served as cofounder, CEO, and chairman of Telecom Technologies, Inc. On September 18, 2006, Anousheh became the first female private space explorer, the fourth private explorer to visit space, and the first astronaut of Iranian descent. She is a member of the X Prize Foundation's Vision Circle as well as its Board of Trustees. She is a life member in the Association of Space Explorers and on the advisory board of the Teachers in Space project.

I immigrated to the United States from Iran, a teenager who didn't speak a word of English. Growing up in Iran, my head was always in the clouds. At night I would spend hours watching the stars, wanting nothing more than to become an astronaut, to fly to space and touch them. My mind was filled with a future where starships would fly to every corner of the universe. I would be the science officer aboard the Starship Enterprise, traveling through wormholes and exploring strange new worlds and new civilizations—to boldly go where no one has gone before. I dreamed of a future with time machines, parallel universes, teleportation and a United Federation of Planets. I was fascinated by all these possibilities because when you're a child, everything is possible—there are no boundaries, and everything is a puzzle to be solved, every dark corner an opportunity for discovery.

When I arrived in the United States, the realities of life put me on a completely different path. I went to school and studied electrical engineering while working full-time. My family moved to the United States with nothing but hopes for a new life and a better future, so finding a job to support myself and my family was important. I found a job at a major telecommunications company, MCI, and started my career as an engineer. Working at MCI was a great experience—I learned the ins and outs of the corporate world while learning a lot about the telecom industry.

President Roosevelt once said: "Far better it is to dare mighty things, to win glorious triumphs, even though checkered by failure, than to rank with those timid spirits who neither enjoy nor suffer much, because they live in the gray twilight that knows neither victory nor defeat." I like to believe that's how I live my life, and so, a few years later, after meeting my husband at MCI, we both left the company and started on our road to entrepreneurship.

Building a company from scratch and growing it is exciting, but also a big challenge. It is very much like raising a child: while it's very rewarding, it also has its share of ups and downs. As a female CEO of a tech company, I learned that even though I lived in one of the most advanced western societies, certain prejudices against women in leadership positions, especially in high tech, still persevered. However, my philosophy has always been to do my best in everything I set my mind to and let my work speak for itself. This has proven to be a most successful strategy and has turned many skeptics into believers and friends.

Although I became a very successful entrepreneur, I still felt that something was missing in my life, and that was my passion for the stars. While I kept my dream alive in my heart and continued to study and learn about space, I wanted to do more. I didn't want to become one of those people who would just complain about what's wrong in this world—I wanted to do something about it and to change it. Sometimes it is easier to take risks when you have very little to lose, but as a successful entrepreneur, taking risks and daring to do big things takes on a whole new meaning. I think most people in my shoes would have given up on their so-called crazy dream and stayed in their comfort zone instead of stepping out and facing uncertainty and potential failure. But for me, it wasn't just a dream. It was a burning passion that gave me a sense of purpose and direction in life.

I've always believed that if you want something bad enough in your heart, the universe conspires to help you achieve it. I consider myself a very lucky person, as one of the few who is living out a childhood dream, but as Louis Pasteur said: "Chance favors a prepared mind." For me, a series of fortunate events led me to Star City, Moscow, and ultimately, to the stars.

It all started with meeting Peter Diamandis, the founder of X Prize Foundation. He is, like me, crazy about outer space, and wanted to do something about opening up access to space. Peter had launched a $10 million competition for anyone not affiliated with a government agency to build a spaceship that could go to space twice within two weeks. It sounded crazy, but to me it was the first opportunity to be part of changing the future for millions of people who shared my dream of space travel.

Peter came to visit us and tell us about his prize, and without hesitation, we saw the value in what he was doing and partnered up with him. The prize was launched as the Ansari X Prize and had twenty-six teams competing from seven countries, each with their own unique and innovative approach on how they would reach one hundred kilometers into space. Ultimately, in a great historic moment, the team from Mojave Aerospace won the prize in October of 2004. After their success, no one would ever again question the power of a small group of focused innovators to achieve seemingly impossible tasks.

On that same day, Virgin Galactic was born, and we knew that our goal of launching a new industry was achieved. Many changes have occurred as a result of the prize, as well as all of the regulatory reform that came from our efforts with the X Prize. NASA started warming up to partnership with small private companies as well as using incentive prizes to bring a wide range of innovative approaches to solve many technical challenges.

On the first anniversary of the Ansari X Prize, I got an invitation to go learn about the Russian space program and train as a backup. I couldn't have been happier. Even though it was one of the coldest winters in Moscow, I didn't care. This was my chance to be part of the space program and get one step closer to my dream. Many people told me I was crazy—that I'd freeze in the Moscow winter, that training on a Russian military base alone was not safe. They even questioned my sanity, but I didn't care. I was like a kid in a candy store: I couldn't wait to get on the plane and meet all of the astronauts and cosmonauts in person, to walk in the hallways where Yuri Gagarin walked, to visit where Tereshkova—the first woman in space—prepared for her historic mission. To me, this was the opportunity of a lifetime, and I would not miss it.

So I went and trained as hard as I could. I was faced with some resistance when I first arrived in Star City, but after a couple of months of hard work, when they realized how serious I was about my training and how passionate I was, all of the instructors became my best friends and advocates. I worked tirelessly and trained for nine months as a backup for a Russian Soyuz mission to the International Space Station—and just three weeks before the flight, I was told that a primary crew member failed one of his medical exams and that I could take his seat.

I spent eleven glorious days in space. I saw Earth as a beautiful blue ball in the vast velvety darkness of space and felt its warmth and energy. I saw a sunset and a sunrise every ninety minutes, and billions of shining stars surrounded us.

There is nothing else like it out there. When you look at Earth from above, you have a new perspective. You can see how insignificant we are compared to the universe that surrounds us, and even more, how insignificant the things we fight over are. Floating in space, from my safe haven among the stars, I saw a world without division—just one Earth—in a vast universe. From my vantage point, the boundary lines separating countries and people had become blurred and then invisible. I knew that back on Earth these imaginary lines were very much present and causing all sorts of problems—but up there, the lines did not matter, did not exist.

Back on Earth, I am focused on my new company, Prodea Systems, which was launched on the same day I launched into space. At Prodea, we are trying to change how people use technology and make it easy and seamless so everyone, from any place, using any device, can enjoy and benefit from the use of technology. As I work to bring this to people all over the world, I am constantly reminded of that beautiful image of our planet and how we are all the same, with similar wants and needs.

In parallel, through my work with the X Prize Foundation and other organizations, I continue to make space more accessible to everyone so that anyone who wants to can have the opportunity to experience what I experienced. I want to make access to space safe and inexpensive so that we can fully benefit from the resources in space to better our lives here on Earth. We have also expanded the use of incentive prizes to solve the biggest challenges humanity faces. Whether at the bottom of the ocean or out in space, in the smallest building block of our bodies or the depth of the sun, we're turning every challenge into an opportunity to advance human life and make our planet a better place for all of us to live together.

We live in a unique time, one that may become a pivotal point in the history of mankind. As humans, never before have we had so much potential to build or to destroy, to grow and seed the universe with our species or to annihilate, to give life or propagate death. Over centuries we have mastered skills and technologies that have given us enormous individual power and shrunk time and space between us, but with great power comes great responsibility, and we must use our imaginations to take risks, break all the boundaries, and challenge the status quo. We cannot be afraid because fear is death—a life in fear is a life not lived. Take it from someone who has been all the way down in the gutter and all the way up to the stars, someone who has gone from one high to a new low and then back up again. The journey is life, and how we live it is our choice. Let's make the journey worthwhile.

CHAPTER 12
WE ARE THE ONES WE'VE BEEN WAITING FOR

MARY GROVE AND MEGAN SMITH

Mary Grove is Google's Director of Global Entrepreneurship Outreach where she leads Google for Entrepreneurs, the company's programs and partnerships to support startups and entrepreneurs in more than 100 countries around the world. Mary earned her BA and MA from Stanford University and sits on the Alumni Association Board of Directors. She is passionate about building community and has led exploratory outreach for Google and work with entrepreneurs for Google in Pakistan, Iraq, Gaza, and Afghanistan. She serves on the Board of UP Global and is the cofounder of Silicon North Stars, an organization that connects youth from the Midwest with Silicon Valley and exposure to careers in tech.

Megan Smith is an entrepreneur, tech evangelist, engineer, catalyst and connector. At Google[x], Megan works on a range of projects, including cocreating/hosting SolveForX and cocreating WomenTechmakers. She was VP of new business development across Google's global engineering and product teams for nine years—including leading acquisitions for Google Earth, Google Maps, and Picasa, and GMing Google.org's engineering transition, adding Google Crisis Response, Google for Nonprofits, Earth Outreach/Engine, and increased employee engagement. Prior to joining Google, Megan was CEO and earlier, COO of PlanetOut and was early at General Magic and Apple Japan. She holds bachelor's and master's degrees in mechanical engineering from MIT, where she now serves on the board. She completed her master's thesis work at the MIT Media Lab.

"I am not an advocate for frequent changes in laws and constitutions, but laws and institutions must go hand in hand with the progress of the human mind. As that becomes more developed, more enlightened, as new discoveries are made, new truths discovered and manners and opinions change, with the change of circumstances, institutions must advance also to keep pace with the times. We might as well require a man [person] to wear still the coat which fitted him when a boy [child] as civilized society to remain ever under the regimen of their barbarous ancestors."

—Thomas Jefferson, July 1816
(displayed at the Jefferson Memorial)

All of us have inherited from history great gifts, innovations, wonderful culture, and sadly, extraordinary biases—both conscious and unconscious.

Today, the vast majority of gender bias is unconscious. The Equality Challenge Unit has shared extensive research about the nature and effect of bias; for example, our unconscious brain processes large amounts of information and looks for patterns 200,000 times faster than the conscious brain, and when it sees patterns occurring together (like seeing men alone in senior leadership), it wires those thoughts together neurally.

As we become much more aware of and educated about the complexities of these biases, how they operate, and the pain and extraordinary economic, cultural, political, creative, and social loss they cause for humanity, it's our responsibility to act, to shift, to upgrade. None of us created these problems, but we can be the ones to make a huge push to fix them.

The gender gap is very real. If we quickly look at just the

United States, we know that women make up 14 percent of Fortune 500 Executive Committees, 17 percent of Congress, and 11 percent of CEO/founder positions of U.S. firms backed by venture capital. These numbers vary by country around the world, but in most cases they are sadly similar or worse, and only on rare exception are they better. The treatment of women varies by country, including extreme regions where women are basically treated as property, places where nearly all of the sixteen points voiced in the historic *Declaration of Sentiments*, created at the world's first Women's Rights Convention in 1848 at Seneca Falls, are still operating culturally and often legally. (If you haven't already, the *Declaration of Sentiments* is worth reading to reflect on how far we have and have not come since the mid-1800s.)

For most of history, the vast majority of people were exposed to and became comfortable with a disparate reality for men and women. In every generation, there have been giants, both women and men, who have worked tirelessly for gender equality—but they faced, and still face, a constant uphill battle.

Today it feels like we're at a tipping point in many parts of the world, where a growing majority of people are conscious of the need for women's equal rights for so many reasons—that we are perhaps about to accelerate on our path to real, meaningful, and lasting gender equality. Activists, artists, and change makers everywhere continue to build upon centuries of incredible work, now that the Internet has dramatically expanded their reach and voice. Conversations abound about the empowerment of women and girls—moved from the sidelines to the center stage at the UN, across developed and developing countries. Sheryl Sandberg's book, *Lean In*, has provoked greater dialogue across professional sectors, and research firms like McKinsey and Catalyst, alongside business schools like Kellogg, Harvard, and MIT, are doing the research we have long needed that shows why it's economically valuable to have gender-inclusive and balanced teams, and how unconscious bias is operating everywhere to block progress. Long-standing groups who work for gender equality in technology fields, like National Center for Women

& Information Technology and the Anita Borg Institute, are getting much more mainstream access to senior executives and others to help educate for change. Research now proves that gender-diverse teams and leadership make better products, companies, organizations, families, communities, and countries.

People across the world responded to the idea Vivek, Tavinder, Farai, Neesha, and their team had to collaboratively create this book—hundreds of women were able to efficiently contribute their personal stories. These are important accounts of their own difficult experiences with the real and perceptual historic biases we have inherited and how they are moving to write our next chapter. Thank you to everyone who has shared useful stories, broad experiences, deeply troubling challenges, success breakthroughs, and critical insights.

Sharing these personal stories and so many more is a big part of the solution.

Making these problems visible through real day-to-day experiences, both the hardship and examples of potential paths forward, show us the hopeless reality and the hopeful ways out.

The stories, the realities that each woman faces, are a powerful way to elicit empathy, allow us to understand much more specifically the challenges, and encourage all of us to look deeper at these issues and evolve.

"'I have always believed that contemporary gender discrimination within universities is part reality and part perception,' MIT President Charles M. Vest wrote in a much-cited preface to the MIT report on gender equity, 'but I now understand that reality is by far the greater part of the balance.'

In 1998, Vest forthrightly acknowledged serious gender equity problems cited by senior women faculty in the School of Science; he then supported corrective measures to address long-standing imbalances. A stunningly candid and publicly released report detailing gender inequity at MIT—and Vest's subsequent leadership on the issue—stimulated the examination of gender equality at universities across the country." (excerpt

MIT News Office)

This study measured a broad range of areas where female faculty faced discrimination; one of the simple examples was measuring lab space for women against men on the faculty over time; the data showed irrefutable discrimination.

This isn't only an issue in the workplace. The Geena Davis Institute on Gender in Media, a 2013 Google Global Impact Grant winner, has done an important job of cataloguing the representation of girls and women in mainstream media with a focus on family and children's media—and the results are pretty bleak.

While women comprise half of the labor pool and hold roughly 30 percent of STEM jobs in the United States, less than 21 percent of female characters in family films, primetime programs, or children's shows are working in STEM fields. For computer science jobs, the ratios were even more extreme, at fifteen males for every female depicted. And we know that visibility matters.

There is an abundance of research showing that seeing very few people like oneself represented in a profession leads all people, but girls and students of color in particular, to feel less welcome, to feel more stress and anxiety than more gender- or race-balanced professions, and to experience debilitating performance pressure. This ultimately means fewer of them pursue computer science as a field or persist with the career once they are there.

> *"If you go alone, you can go fast. If you go together, you can go far."*
>
> *—African proverb*

Solutions are coming faster because people are working in parallel globally—the surface area of people who are waking up to the issues, who care and are doing something about the problem, has drastically increased. And we need many more people to do the same, see the issues and act, do what they can.

Actions we can take today fall into two buckets: things that are actionable now, and areas we need to debug, where we don't know what to do or even what's causing the issues.

There are many things we can do right now as people, as organizations, as leaders, as parents, as media professionals, as teachers, as women, as men—things that we know work or look incredibly promising. Many are listed in this book. Take the time to find out about so many of these solutions that work that you can implement now. Develop the will to get these done; act at scale.

For areas we need to uncover, we need to ask simple and hard questions, explore, iterate, research, try pilot ideas, and work to debug those—then scale and solve further. Let's start this harder work.

We are more hopeful about the future than ever before, and we know that with a roadmap and tools to empower us and elevate our work as a community, with ourselves and some great allies, we can accelerate progress.

The Internet is democratizing entrepreneurship of all kinds (social, commercial, and political); costs have decreased rapidly while access is increasing rapidly. The web has opened up access to global markets with global competition from day one. Entrepreneurship is thriving in communities all over the world. New models have emerged, like crowdfunding (how this book was created and funded), that enable us to build and create and reach new audiences directly. These are still very early days— sometimes we call them "Model T" days—but we can really see the extraordinary global shift.

The acceleration of interconnection is creating a global community of communities, from the spread of ideas worth spreading through TEDx and the network of Google Developer Groups in more than one hundred countries (all run by tech enthusiasts and community leaders), to the rise of tech hubs gathering innovators locally, coworking spaces, and tech accelerators across the globe. This strong desire to have a sense of community, to be a part of the global conversation, and act, fueled by the Internet, has changed the game.

It's interesting to reflect back to 1848 Seneca Falls—a "network" was part of the gathering. At the time, that network was the Erie Canal, which, like the Silk Route and other important commercial trade networks, was also an important route for the exchange of ideas and for ideas to travel. Many of the ideas of women's rights and suffrage, as well as abolition, were part of the conversations that evolved from the movement of goods with people along the Erie Canal.

Around the world, leaders have been present for all time, but the network is now enabling so many more to emerge on the global stage. Organizations like Vital Voices, Global Fund for Women, Global Fund for Children, Ashoka, TED Fellows, Skoll Fellows, Astia, and Endeavor are finding extraordinary talent to accelerate, talk about, and invest in; women and men are solving serious local and global problems in the area of trafficking, security, peace, agriculture, energy, civil society representation, civil rights, education, and more.

In technology specifically, organizations have grown and new ones have emerged who are networking and engaging talent, from youth programs like GirlsWhoCode, BlackGirlsWhoCode, Code.org, scratch.mit.edu, MadeWithCode.com, and FIRSTRobotics to professional groups like the NewMe Accelerator and VC outreach to women like the consciousness efforts of Andreessen Horowitz. Long-standing programs like Systers from ABI and new programs and places like Women Techmakers, Women Who Code, Double Union, and many more are growing.

People make change possible—change does not just happen—and so using the Silicon Valley approach, believing in and supporting talented entrepreneurs to make changes happen and innovate, will serve us well. We need to see and support the extraordinary emerging talent globally—women and men who have incredible solutions that can work.

> *"Women have always been an equal part of the past, just not an equal part of history."*
>
> —*Gloria Steinem*

Attending the annual Grace Hopper Celebration, the largest regular gathering of technical women, changes perspectives about what's possible. Once you see the five thousand technical women the gathering brings together, you realize the talent is here and we can improve our industry.

With nearly sixteen million programmers in the world, at 10 to 15 percent women, there are more than two million women programmers—but we never see them. Technical women remain largely invisible and behind the scenes despite important and often elite contributions.

In tech, we are standing on the shoulders of giants—men and women who have innovated and collaborated to bring us to where we are today. So many entrepreneurs, computer scientists, heroes, and creators have come before us—and yet we are critically challenged by the lack of visibility of the technical women and minorities who are and have been an elite part of our field in both the past and present. Here are just a few examples from history:

- U.S. Navy Rear Admiral Grace Hopper, for whom the celebration is named, developed the first compiler and conceptualized the whole idea of machine-independent programming languages.
- More than half of the mathematicians at Bletchley Park who broke the ENIGMA codes during World War II were women—a team credited with shortening World War II by two years and saving eleven million lives.
- The original "computers" were women—one group at the University of Pennsylvania had more than eighty women mathematicians brought together to calculate ballistic trajectories during World War II. Six were recruited to become America's first digital programmers—for the ENIAC project. They were the first modern programmers in U.S. history.
- NASA's Katherine Johnson calculated the trajectories for Alan Shepard, John Glenn, and the Apollo Mission and coauthored more than twenty-six technical papers

at NASA—but due to discriminatory policy in the day, her name only appears on one.

- Of course, Ada Lovelace, who was the first person in the world to write about the idea, discovered programmability in mid-1843.
- And more—there are hundreds of historic and current examples of women and minorities doing groundbreaking work in technology, but many of these stories are not well-known, and in some cases, the stories have been all but lost.

We need to know these names like we know the male innovators of those days.

In the Hollywood film *Jobs*, all of the men on the core Macintosh team are introduced and have speaking roles, but we don't meet Joanna Hoffman or Susan Kare, though both were a core part of the original Macintosh product development team, and their contributions literally changed the face of the Mac and our industry. In the Turing films, we rarely meet the many female code-breakers at Bletchley Park. The list goes on and on—in historic and contemporary movies about our industry, the women are typically written as love interests, with technical women rarely appearing as core contributors. Science fiction movies paint the same gender-imbalanced future, and few movies overall pass the Bechdel Test: having two named, female characters speak to each other about something other than a man.

The Geena Davis Institute on Gender in Media (GDI), mentioned earlier in the chapter, through studies done with the USC Annenberg School, found a three to one ratio of male to female characters in children's TV, with 80 percent of the jobs held by characters in kids TV and films being held by male characters. We need to help Hollywood and other media creation hubs fix this damaging bug. Armed with GDI research and the need to shift, we and many others have begun helping with outreach work to top media partners. We are also helping the GDI team leverage digital technology advances to enhance the tools used to measure gender imbalance in children's media to shine a light on the realities.

We have been working through Women Techmakers to increase the visibility of technical women, in addition to community and resource access in our developer events like Google IO and Google Developer Groups around the world. This year we moved from 8 percent women attendees to more than 20 percent by taking the time to work on outreach to technical women who should be attending, but were opting to not come. We have added unconscious bias training for all speakers at our IO event. Events like Women 2.0, Hopper, BlogHer, IWD Programs, and many others are helping connect technical women and raise visibility. Online, the Makers.com website now has the largest collection of stories about women—and the technology and science section is slowly filling up with women who everyone should know about. Makers is coming out with five films this year—Women in Space, Politics, War, Comedy, and Hollywood—in addition to their groundbreaking PBS series completed in 2013. These films change perspectives, perceptions, and the baseline for people.

There are great resources emerging for action here—other parts of this book have outlined specific actions individuals and organizations should be taking to better advance women in our field and also improved hiring practices. We have a tremendous opportunity to help change the narrative and our actions—all of us, women and men working alongside one another, have an important role to play here.

As employers, we can attract, hire, and retain outstanding women. At Google, for example, our goal is to build technology that helps people change the world, and we're more likely to succeed if Google reflects the diversity of our users. Like other companies, we have created internal support networks and communities; women learned from being part of the Women@ Google global network of more than four thousand women Googlers across more than twenty-seven countries.

As leaders of teams, we can highlight ways to make working parents' lives a little easier. Think about what benefit programs you advocate for, what flexible work environments you can create. One of our favorite programs is at Google's Campus Tel Aviv and Campus London spaces for the startup communities. The team there has developed Campus for Moms, a spin on the traditional tech accelerator; new moms looking to launch products and build companies come through a formal program, but meet once a week and bring their babies with them. There are play areas and feeding rooms, and everyone builds together. The result is astounding and proof that we can break through the traditional ceilings and walls that exist in our old models.

As individuals, we can mix curiosity for learning with strong, sustained confidence in ourselves to know that we are capable of tremendous achievement. Don't be afraid to ask for help, to know what you don't know, to seek out mentorship and role models you respect. We have both been helped tremendously throughout our career by amazing mentors, both male and female (Mary cites Megan as one of the most influential mentors in her life). Seek them out. And when you're in a position to be able to give back and do the same, pay it forward wholeheartedly.

We also need to be careful as an industry not to think the issue is fixing women—the issue is fixing our tech culture, upgrading our tech culture to be much more welcoming of underrepresented people, to be better.

When Lou Gerstner took the helm at IBM in the 1990s, he structured his management team in a way that they could help underrepresented groups at IBM thrive. He gave the leadership team much better access to understand the challenges of these members of IBM, even if they were not yet a diverse leadership team. He had each of his direct reports work directly with the eight employee resource groups at IBM—and he asked the IBMers how to find more employees, suppliers, and customers from their group and how to best help them thrive and grow at IBM. This shift helped IBM work on their challenges and adapt culture to the groups and individuals, not ask them to change.[70]

There are three areas where there are many inexpensive and

---

[70] David A. Thomas, "IBM Finds Profit in Diversity." *Working Knowledge*, September 27, 2004. http://hbswk.hbs.edu/item/4389.html

scalable things we can do today to accelerate progress. These areas are:

- Internet and mobile network access that opens up opportunity and draws in our other 4 billion colleagues online and into the conversation
- Access in terms of training and internetworking our colleagues today who are not yet part of the digital economy and conversation
- Building a broad pipeline of talent with STEAM (Science, Technology, Engineering, Math, and Arts and Design) with our young generation

There are inexpensive and scalable things we can do today to accelerate progress in each of these three areas.

Many examples of this in action surround us. In 2011, we visited both Kabul and Herat in Afghanistan and met with Internet service providers, mobile operators, students, developers, journalists, and entrepreneurs. In Afghanistan, 60 percent of the population is under the age of twenty, and tremendous challenges exist alongside tremendous opportunity. We met dozens of young computer science students, who were fired up to share their ideas with us and why Google should build them. We felt excited when the U.S. Department of Defense launched an incubator near Herat University because we could help support and empower these young entrepreneurs to build these companies themselves. The first graduate of the program, Roya Mahboob, runs one of the largest software companies in Afghanistan, proudly employing many women, and serving as an inspiration to young aspiring talent. In 2013, *Time* magazine named Roya one of the most influential people in the world.

> *"Few will have the greatness to bend history itself; but each of us can work to change a small portion of events, and in the total; of all those acts will be written the history of this generation."*
>
> —*Robert Kennedy*

We see two important opportunities for the future here:

The first is championing and supporting organizations whose direct mission is to support women. Organizations like Astia, Women 2.0, Vital Voices, the Global Fund for Women, and UP Global are working directly to ensure more women have access to the opportunities they deserve. We both sit on the boards of some of these organizations and are fortunate to witness firsthand how tremendous leadership in action can lead to direct results.

In June 2013, UP Global hosted the Startup Weekend Women's Edition SF and, with 85 percent women, clocked in with the highest number of women ever at a startup weekend. Many shared how they had long considered participating in a startup weekend event, but once they heard that one was specifically for female entrepreneurs, they jumped at the opportunity and never looked back. UP Global is working on a new initiative with support from Google for Entrepreneurs and Blackstone Foundation called Startup Women, an effort to increase participation of women across UP Global's programs and help 1,500 women-led startups launch this year.

The second layer is thinking about increasing diversity as a thin underlay across all the work we do globally. We saw this with Manos Accelerator, a new tech accelerator for Latino startup founders; they made a conscious decision to ensure they filled their pipeline with both male and female founders, and subsequently their first class of startups featured five of the seven teams with a female founder. Google for Entrepreneurs launched the global #40Forward effort this year to increase representation of women in forty startup communities with forty partners. Organizations did everything from simply tweak the time of day of their events to launch women-focused accelerators. It's not just about one organization or one community—the ideas is to shift the way we think about inclusion across the board.

There is enormous potential to tackle the world's toughest challenges with women and men working together on solutions, tremendous opportunity to improve our communities and our countries and together to elevate our global human condition through entrepreneurship and "10X thinking." It requires courage, rolling up our sleeves, and moving outside of our comfort zone and our traditional ways of thinking.

Gloria Steinem said, "Don't think about making women fit the world—think about making the world fit women." As an industry, we are just at the start of understanding this insight and how we might change and adapt our tech culture to better accommodate so many more innovators.

If not now, when? If not us, who? Take action.

We are the ones we've been waiting for.

ENDNOTE
AN ODE TO WOMEN LIKE YOU TRANSFORMING THE WORLD

FARAI CHIDEYA

During one of the many recent battles over gender and technology companies, a series of comments online repeated the same message. Tech has done just fine without a lot of women around; maybe better than if they had been. How can you fault companies for being successful *without* women at the top? Isn't that punishing success?

First, as Megan Smith of Google points out, the true story of women in science, technology, and innovation has not been told. Adding women to leadership teams and boards has had a measurably positive effect on growth and success. Don't corporations have a fiduciary duty to maximize investor value? And if women add value, isn't it poor leadership to ignore the fiscal upside of gender diversity? There have been and are many more women in medical sciences, space innovation, engineering, and design, just to name a few fields, than get their due.

The same facile arguments about why the world doesn't need women get made over and over again. Some of it is ignorance, some of it is hostility, and some of it, I daresay, is the limited roster of people who have come to epitomize success. We haven't yet seen a female Steve Jobs—a person who has crossed over from the realm of technical and business innovation into pop culture icon status. So, one way to think about changing the game is to hope for, wish for, or *become* the next Jobs. Another way—and I'd argue a more profound long-term strategy—is to seek to redefine the way we identify and elevate trailblazers. After all, the dizzying number of stories we have told (not to mention all the ones we didn't have space for) break down the myth that there is only one way to be a female leader.

Take credit for your work. Don't let anyone tell you that you are too bold or too "pushy" (a term applied often to strong women) when you demand the same respect a man would get for similar work. Seek every ally you can find because success is rooted not only in performance but perception. And realize that in the long run, there are many ways to shine. Like many of you, I mentor. I helped a former student of mine, then a double major in political science and computer science, get a job as a data-driven journalist—a world that allows her to use all her passions and skills. She wrote me excitedly about being invited to an international coding conference and then said, "I wouldn't be here without you." Ask yourself, during the good times and especially during the hard ones, how many people wouldn't be here without *you?* Hold tight to not just your own victories, but those you have helped others achieve.

At some point, you have to make peace with this flawed world of ours. That does not mean accepting injustice (gender-based or otherwise), but rather acknowledging its existence and persistence. One story in the Buddhist tradition has a demon, Mara, repeatedly working to undermine and tempt the Buddha on his way to enlightenment. Even after the Buddha reached enlightenment, Mara didn't go away. He'd skulk around from time to time, and the Buddha's right-hand man tried to keep the demon away. But the Buddha told his friend to calm down and called out, "I see you, Mara. Would you like some tea?" The act of acknowledging that the demon was there—and even inviting him to the table—stripped Mara of his power to inspire fear.

Everyday demons like gender bias will raise their heads again and again, but how we react can change. We can change how much we feel empowered to act in our collective interest and adapt new strategies to the workplace and work/family/

life synergy. *Innovating Women* is full of collective wisdom about how to be a leader while raising children, to start a career strong, to deal with adversity and, yes, with the people who underestimate women's power. The fact that women will have to continue to fight for our place in the world shouldn't inspire fear. We are winning—perhaps more slowly than we'd like, but triumphing nonetheless.

So the next time you run into someone who just doesn't get it or, worse, is actively part of the gender problem, you can metaphorically (or even literally) invite them to tea. Let them realize that the world holds far more opportunity for everyone with women fully vested in science, technology, and innovation; that success is not a zero sum game. All of us deserve a world where the power of women is unleashed and unbound and where the virtuous circle of innovating women's creativity and brilliance helps us all.

ACKNOWLEDGMENTS

In the 1730s, a brilliant female mathematician, Emilie du Châtelet, translated and popularized Sir Isaac Newton's arcane *Principia Mathematica*, inspired Voltaire's writings, and created the foundation for Einstein to develop his theories.[71] But few have heard of her. Similarly, a century later, Marie Curie performed pioneering research on radioactivity and won two Nobel prizes—yet she is hardly known to Americans.

These are just two of thousands of examples of great women in every country of the world. Rarely have women been recognized for their achievements.

This book is dedicated to these women—who made the world a better place with their contributions to the sciences, engineering, arts, and the humanities. And it is a tribute to many others who will soon help solve humanity's greatest challenges.

Our special thanks to the hundreds of women who helped us with research and ideas and told their personal stories, to the hundreds of men and women who helped fund our crowdfunded campaign, and to the Kauffman Foundation, Stanford Law School, Pratt School of Engineering at Duke University, Google for Entrepreneurs, Xerox corporation, Women 2.0, National Center for Women & Information Technology, Anita Borg Institute, Level Playing Field Institute, and Indiegogo.

Thank you to Neesha Bapat for being a great leader and managing this project. Neesha also led the research that preceded this and worked with our partner organizations. And thanks to Kristen Van Nest for her writing contribution, research,

[71] David Bodanis, *Passionate Minds: The Great Love Affair of the Enlightenment*, http://www.amazon.com/Passionate-Minds-Enlightenment-Featuring-Scientist/dp/0307237206.

and commitment to capturing the voices and stories of these amazing women.

A special thanks to the most innovative woman in publishing: our literary agent Kathleen Anderson. She has been incredible in navigating the old and new worlds of publishing and bringing this project together.

No doubt we will miss many, but here are the names of some of the innovating women who contributed content to this book and helped as our ambassadors.

Yinka Abdu	Maura Adamczyk	Cynthia. F Adkins
Frances Advincula	Ana Alonso	Daniella Alpher
Terri Anderson	Anousheh Ansari	Jennifer Argüello
Manjiri Bakre	Chithralekha Balamurugan	Pam Barry
Nandini Barua	Susan Baxter	Christina Baylcoq
Stephanie Belawicz	Brooks Bell	Lisa Nicole Bell
Kristina Bennin	Srijata Bhatnagar	Jagruti Bhikha
Beth Blechermen	Angelika Blendstrup	Keely Brandon
Jodie Brinkerhoff	Simone Brummelhuis	Amrita C Aviyente
Cecilia Castillo	Claudia Chan	Sovita Chander
Yuliana Chandra	Shaherose Charania	Judy Chen
Shikha Chhatpar	Farai Chideya	Ayelet Co-Ideate
Nancy Conrad	Carolina Dams	Joséphine de Chazournes
Christine DeFilippo	Stacy Donohue	Tasha Drew
Lisa Dusseault	Katie Elizabeth	Baat Enosh
Ghalia Farzat	Ellen Feaheny	Emily Fowler
Grace Francisco	Marcia Gadbois	Nolwenn Godard
Anita Goel	Francine Gordon	Sarah Granger
Mary Grove	Megan Groves	Melissa Hardway
Anne Hartley	Bobbilee Hartman	Kristina Hathaway
Linda Hayes	Cynthia Hellen	Kirstie Hepburn
Evonne Heyning	Julia Hoey	Emily Holdman

Alja Isakovic · Alicia Ismach · Deborah Jackson

Leticia Jáuregui Casanueva · Whitney Johnson · Quendrith Johnson

S. Mitra Kalita · Purti Kanodia · Kavita Kapur

Laura Karolchik-Griffin · Suzanna Keith · Kausar Khizra

Regina Knaster · Anna Kojzar · Kay Koplovitz

Christine Kraft · Lauren Kritzer · Angela Kyle

Deepa Lalla · Michelle Lara Lin · Ellen Leanse

Angela Lee Foreman · Jocelyn Leon · Samia Lounis

TD Lowe · Shannon Lucas · Saru Mahajan

Kareen Mallet · Geeta Manjunath · Lisa Marie Martinez

Laura Mather · Maya Mathias · Sarah McBride

Melissa McCoy · Hamutal Meridor · Deborah Mills-Scofield

Angela Min · Sian Morson · Carrie-Anne Mosley

Diane Murphy · Jex Musa · Deepa Muthukrishnan

Britta Muzyk · Jen Myronuk · Anne Neville

Danielle Newman · Van Trinh Nguyen · Fiona Nielsen

Rashmi Nigam · Nathalie Niño · Kristy O'Driscoll

Victoria Oldridge · Rachel Olsen · Priscilla Oppenheimer

Shabnam Ozlati · Karen Palmer · Natalie Panek

Phaedra Pardue · Priyanka Pathak · Ellen Pearlman

Kathryn Pellegrini · Kim Polese · Prasita Prabhakaran

Lakshmi Pratury · Nathalie Prouvost · Virgilia Pruthi

Nasa Quba · Anjali Ramachandran · Jessica Ramirez

Patricia Rangel · Sara Rao · Alice Rathjen

Katherine Read · Stephanie Redivo · Ana Redmond

Allannah Rodrigues-Smith · Heidi Roizen · Catherine Rose

Carolina Rossi · Deb Rothschild · Jennifer Ryan

Irina Rymshina · Merline Saintil · Kristen Sanderson

Jyoti Sarin · Agustina Sartori · Lisa Marie Schaefer

Cynthia Schames   Beth Schecter   Pascale Scheurer
Sara Scoville-   Stephen Sequenzia   Silvija Seres
Weaver
Maria Shamuel   Kirti Sharma   Shazia Siddiqi
Linda Simovic   Melissa Simpler   Lori Skagen Mehen
Megan Smith   Sujata Srinivasan   Anne Stenros
Alese Stroud   Sectha Sundaresan   Mary Taylor
Babette Ten Haken Maria Theodoulou   Maria Thompson
Lynn Tilton   Ida Tin   Bhramara Tirupati
Michael Topolovac Charity Tran   Cynthia Trevino
Barbara Troncoso   Kristin Valente   Aparna Vedapuri
                                       Singh
Pragati Verma   Natasha Vincent   Kelly Vucovich
Nell Watson   Bianca Welds   Joy Williams
Suxia Yang   Feben Yohannes   Martha Zimet

As well as the innovating men who contributed to our efforts.

Paresh Ghelani   Timothy Coleman   Peter Diamandis
Joel Dudley   Bradley Feld   Peter Gylfe
John. F Harris   David Hepburn   Andrew Hessel
Clarence Irving   Tim Kastelle   Howard Kettner
Joey Neugrat   John O' Loughlin   Eric Reis
Nathan Ryan   Stephen Sequenzia   Douglas Standley
Michael Topolovac John Warren

VIVEK WADHWA is a Fellow at Arthur & Toni Rembe Rock Center for Corporate Governance, Stanford University; Director of Research at the Center for Entrepreneurship and Research Commercialization at the Pratt School of Engineering, Duke University; and Distinguished Fellow at Singularity University. He is the author of *The Immigrant Exodus: Why America Is Losing the Global Race to Capture Entrepreneurial Talent*, named a Book of the Year of 2012 by *The Economist*. He was named by *Foreign Policy Magazine* as a Top 100 Global Thinker in 2012. In 2013, *TIME* magazine listed him as one of the 40 Most Influential Minds in Tech.

Wadhwa oversees research at Singularity University, which educates a select group of leaders about the exponentially growing technologies that are soon going to change our world.

In his roles at Stanford and Duke, Wadhwa lectures on subjects such as entrepreneurship and public policy, and leads groundbreaking research projects. He is an advisor to several governments; mentors entrepreneurs; and is a regular columnist for *The Washington Post, Wall Street Journal Accelerators*, LinkedIn Influencers blog, *Forbes*, and the American Society of Engineering Education's *Prism* magazine. Prior to joining academia in 2005, Wadhwa founded two software companies.

FARAI CHIDEYA brings the human experience alive in media. A fiction and non-fiction author, reporter, and broadcaster, she has interviewed business innovators and politicians; white supremacists and murderers. She believes that embracing our shared humanity is crucial to journalism. A former on-air reporter and host for ABC News, CNN, and NPR, she recently launched One with Farai, a brand which produces public radio podcasts and broadcast specials; and hosts live events also packaged for broadcast. She is working with a group of entrepreneurs to develop new, sustainable models (public, private, and hybrid) for civic-minded and diverse journalism. Farai is also a Distinguished Writer in Residence at New York University's Arthur L. Carter Journalism Institute.

THANK YOU TO OUR SPONSORS